Short-cut Cookbook

✛

ANNE STIRK

BBC BOOKS

This book is published to accompany the
television series entitled *Bazaar*
which was first broadcast in June 1993
Published by BBC Books,
a division of BBC Enterprises Limited,
Woodlands, 80 Wood Lane
London W12 0TT

First Published 1993
© Anne Stirk 1993
ISBN 0 563 36777 6
Designed by Judith Gordon
Illustrations by Debbie Thompson
Front cover home economist: Ricky Turner
Set in 11pt Ehrhardt by Ace Filmsetting Ltd, Frome
Printed and bound in Great Britain by
Redwood Press Ltd, Melksham
Cover printed by Clays Ltd, St Ives Plc

Contents

Acknowledgements

Many thanks to Nicky Copeland and Erica Griffiths for their helpful advice and support, and to my family, Edward and Sarah and especially Ken, my husband. Thanks to my mum, Alice Burns, my sister Mary Hunt, to Pat Peacock for her help with some of the recipe testing and to Rita Wood. Finally, thanks to ISL Office Services in Easingwold; to Sue and especially Lillian 'Doris' Lund who has tried several recipes 'hot' from her word processor.

Introduction

⁘

I think that this book should really be dedicated to a friend of mine who trained with me at Leeds Polytechnic as a home economics teacher, and who insists that the only short-cut in cookery is a visit to the nearest Marks and Spencer's food hall! If you shop regularly, you can't fail to notice the ever-increasing selection of ready-prepared foods – in fact, you probably ask yourself, as I do, 'what will they think of next?'. There's always some new product on the shelves to try to tempt us into submission. There are ranges of fish products with accompanying sauces, casseroles, pies, puddings, soups, bread and cakes. The increase in foreign travel has also created a demand for ready-prepared exotic dishes from all over the world. Even so, however good these convenience dishes are, they do not have that unmistakeable something which typifies home cooking: real taste and flavour.

This book is not merely about convenience, but short-cuts to real food. There are plenty of fresh seasonal ingredients combined in uncomplicated recipes to create wholesome nourishing dishes. Many traditional recipes can be successfully shortened, many complicated processes can be by-passed or replaced with a technique which gives a faster result. You will find plenty of casseroles, stews, granny's favourite puddings and pies plus some regional favourites. You will find plenty of brand new ideas, too. Some recipes make use of part-baked products which we can cleverly finish off at home – so we don't feel too guilty about taking short-cuts! It seems that this guilt factor is significant when we try to cut corners, so hopefully the legitimate short-cuts suggested in this book will help to assuage some of the guilt.

The other important factor in the convenience food versus real food debate is the health factor. Ready-prepared foods tend to make use of heavily processed ingredients, they are higher in sugar and fat and lower in fibre. You will find that even in the short-cut recipes, the

5

World Health Organization guide-lines on healthy eating are followed where possible. Sugar has not been eliminated completely, but you will find wholemeal flour, skimmed milk, polyunsaturated margarine and olive oil used in many recipes.

Many people associate short-cut cookery with the use of the microwave and you may be surprised that I have not included any microwave recipes. Microwaves do have their place – for example for melting chocolate or gelatine and for defrosting – and they can also successfully cook small quantities of vegetables. However, I do feel that the cooking time is so short that flavours are not allowed to develop and I therefore would not use them for cooking main meals.

With recipes ranging from soups and starters to vegetarian recipes, ideas for light meals and snacks, meat and poultry dishes and plenty of desserts, there should be a short-cut recipe here for everyone.

The Short-cut Store Cupboard

A good store cupboard is invaluable in any kitchen, but if you want to take short-cuts there are a number of special ingredients which are important to have to hand. There is nothing worse than finding you are missing an important ingredient for a recipe when the shops are closed.

HERBS

I tend to use freeze-dried herbs because I feel they have a better colour and flavour. It's a good idea to add one or two varieties to your collection each time you visit the supermarket, but don't store them for too long otherwise they will lose their flavour. If you don't already have a herb rack, here are some of the herbs which you will find useful.

Bay leaves	Parsley
Bouquet garni	Rosemary
Mint	Sage
Mixed herbs	Tarragon
Oregano	Thyme

SPICES

Chilli powder	Nutmeg, ground and whole
Cloves	Paprika
Coriander	Pepper, black and white
Cumin	Peppercorns
Garam masala	Poppy seeds
Ginger	Salt, rock
Mixed spice	Sesame seeds

SAUCES AND FLAVOURINGS

Anchovy essence
Garlic purée
Lemon juice
Mint sauce
Mustard, English and French
Olive oil, extra virgin
Soy sauce
Stock, jar of concentrated vegetable: this is less salty than stock cubes and is available from health food stores
Stock cubes
Tabasco sauce
Tomato purée
Tomatoes, sun-dried: buy a jar of these in olive oil as a special treat to add to casseroles and stews to give a wonderful flavour. If you buy dry sun-dried tomatoes, place them in a screw-top jar and cover with olive oil. Leave until they have softened slightly before using.
Vanilla essence
Vanilla pods
Vegetable oil: I use sunflower oil which is high in polyunsaturates
Vinegar, malt
Wine, red and white
Wine vinegar
Worcestershire sauce

BAKING AND DRY GOODS

Baking powder
Bicarbonate of soda
Cocoa
Dried fruit: no-need-to-soak varieties of apricots, prunes, sultanas, raisins, currants
Drinking chocolate
Flour: wholemeal and white self-raising, wholemeal and white plain
Lentils

Muesli base mix
Oatmeal
Pasta: dried pasta shapes, no-need-to-soak egg or spinach lasagne
Rice: short-grain and long-grain
Sugar: caster, granulated, soft brown, muscovado, icing

TINNED GOODS

Beans: aduki, butter, cannellini, flageolet, haricot, red kidney, soy
Salmon
Tomatoes, tinned: these now come in a selection of flavourings,
    some with herbs, some with garlic, and so on
Tuna

FROZEN GOODS

Ready-made pastry cases
Puff pastry: sheets, blocks and ready-cut pie tops
Rich shortcrust pastry
Shortcrust pastry

MISCELLANEOUS

Butter or margarine: I usually use a margarine which is high in
    polyunsaturates; read the nutritional information on the labels
Milk: I use semi-skimmed milk

Equipment

❖

A cookery book aimed at short-cutting the time spent in the kitchen will obviously rely on a few well chosen gadgets to make the task even easier. Everyone has their favourite piece of time-saving equipment, and mine is the food processor.

Even a fairly basic processor will tackle a whole range of jobs such as slicing, grating, shredding, mincing and puréeing. It will rustle up breadcrumbs in seconds, and will tackle mayonnaise and dressings with ease. Cake-making is also very easy, a twenty-second 'whizz' is often enough time to achieve the correct consistency for your favourite cake.

Although some people swear by the processor for pastry-making, this is one job I prefer to do by hand so I can get the feel of the texture required. The processor is so efficient that it can over-process the margarine and flour, making the addition of the correct amount of water difficult.

After the initial outlay, my processor has more than paid for itself. It is extremely well travelled, having been to various cookery demonstrations and also to the kitchen of our local radio station, BBC Radio York, where I frequently broadcast on a whole range of cookery topics.

Food processors are available in a whole range of sizes and prices but the best advice is: if you do intend to purchase one buy the best you can afford – especially if you do a lot of cooking.

If you don't have a processor, you can purée by rubbing ingredients through a sieve using the back of a spoon.

SMALLER SHORT-CUT EQUIPMENT

Knives: good quality knives to include two small vegetable knives; two cook's knives; palette knife; carving knife; bread knife.

Grater: I find the box-type grater with a range of grating options the most useful.

Lemon zester: one of the most used and useful pieces of equipment in my kitchen. It is perfect for extracting smaller amounts of zest from lemons, limes or oranges and is particularly useful for awkwardly shaped fruit.

Lemon squeezer: plastic or pyrex work equally well.

Cheese parer: enables you to pare off very thin slices of cheese.

Expanding spatula: good for lifting fragile quiches etc. Look out, too, for a useful gadget called an easy lifter – a very thin sheet of aluminium, rather like a small baking sheet, good for lifting cakes, desserts etc., perfect for those occasions when you need two pairs of hands.

Sieves: it's a good idea to have two in different sizes.

Colander: the aluminium ones are more expensive to buy initially but are sturdier and will last longer.

Folding vegetable steamer: opens up rather like a waterlily and fits in most sizes of pans; a very healthy way to cook.

Kitchen scales: even though many experienced cooks can guess at quantities required for recipes, I feel that it is much safer to weigh all your ingredients first.

Measuring jugs: two different sized jugs will be useful.

Saucepans: the choice is endless here, and depending on the size of your family you will need a range of different sized pans. Many people swear by non-stick surfaces on pans, but they quickly become scratched; any non-stick material needs a lot of care.

Although cast-iron enamelled pans are fairly expensive and heavy I do find they cook food very evenly and without burning. It is false economy to buy very light flimsy pans, as you will be constantly disappointed with their performance. Stainless steel pans are also good to use.

Casserole dishes: I use cast-iron enamel casseroles. They cook food beautifully, can be used on the hobs for preparation and you can then continue to cook on the hob or transfer them to the oven.

Quiche tins: these again need to be the heavier duty variety with loose bottoms. A 20 cm/8 in and a 25 cm/10 in tin will give you plenty of choice for cooking for larger or smaller numbers.

Baking sheets: buy two or three heavy duty sheets especially if you are cooking biscuits and scones.

Loaf tins: there are a good selection available and they are useful for the all-in-one recipes in the Baking section. You will find 450 g/1 lb and 900 g/2 lb tins useful to have.

Electric whisk: an electric hand whisk is a boon if you want to make the all-in-one recipes in this book. They are relatively inexpensive and will more than pay for themselves in the time you will save.

Whisks: I find a flat whisk and a balloon whisk very useful, especially for whisking up all-in-one sauces.

The list of equipment is by no means exhaustive but hopefully will serve as a guide to useful equipment to help with the recipes in this book.

Notes on the Recipes

1 Follow one set of measurements only, do not mix metric and Imperial.
2 Eggs are size 3
3 Wash fresh produce before preparation.
4 Spoon measurements are level.
5 Adjust seasoning and strongly-flavoured ingredients, such as onions and garlic, to suit your own taste.

Soups and Starters

I do enjoy having friends around for a meal, whether it's a simple supper or more of a special occasion, where three or four courses are called for. I find that people prefer a starter which is light and I certainly look to recipes which are easily prepared in advance. All the recipes in this chapter could also be served as a light lunch or as a snack.

Home-made soups are delicious and wholesome and they are also very healthy, making use of fresh seasonal ingredients. It is not necessary to make a home-made stock if the main ingredients are robustly flavoured. If you have a blender or a processor you can whizz up a creamy puréed soup very speedily, such as Carrot and Orange Soup (page 22) and Borscht (page 15).

I have also included a couple of quick dips in this section, making use of the convenient tinned beans, to serve with fingers of crunchy vegetables such as courgettes, carrots, red or green peppers and cucumber.

Pâtés are always a popular starter but normally require long slow cooking. There are short-cuts, however, and I have included a tasty fish pâté and a chicken pâté, both of which by-pass the more traditional and lengthy process.

Bean and Parsley Dip

❖

A tasty dip using the convenient tinned beans which don't need to be soaked overnight and then boiled as do dried beans. Do remember, though, if you do soak your own beans, you must boil them hard for 10 minutes during cooking to eliminate the toxins present. If you use canned beans you won't have to bother with all that.

SERVES 4

1 × 425 g (15 oz) tin kidney beans, drained and rinsed
2 tablespoons lemon juice
6 tablespoons olive oil
2 cloves garlic, peeled and crushed

1 tablespoon fresh parsley, finely chopped
Salt and freshly ground black pepper
3 rashers streaky bacon, de-rinded

Place the kidney beans, lemon juice, olive oil, garlic, parsley, salt and pepper in a food processor or blender and process until smooth. Transfer to a suitable container. Grill the bacon until very crisp then crumble over the surface of the dip. Serve with pitta bread or strips of courgette, carrot, pepper, cucumber or other vegetables.

This recipe is not suitable for freezing.

Hummus

❖

Hummus has become a popular dip to serve at parties. It is made with chick peas, and many people swear by the lengthy process of soaking them overnight, followed by lengthy boiling. I find all this unnecessary, preferring to short-cut the traditional process by using tinned chick peas.

SERVES 4

1 × 425 g (15 oz) tin chick
 peas, drained and rinsed
2 tablespoons water
Juice of 1½ lemons
1–2 cloves garlic, peeled and
 crushed

2–3 tablespoons tahini
 (sesame seed paste)
6 tablespoons olive oil
Salt and freshly ground
 black pepper

FOR THE GARNISH

Ground paprika

Fresh coriander leaves

Place the chick peas in a food processor or blender with the water, lemon juice and garlic. Process until a smooth purée is formed. Add the tahini and process again briefly. With the motor of the processor running, gradually drizzle in 5½ tablespoons of the oil in a steady stream. Season to taste with salt and pepper and spoon into a serving dish. To prevent the hummus from drying out you can spoon the remaining oil on top. Cover with foil or cling-film and chill until required. Garnish with a sprinkling of paprika and the fresh coriander and serve with warm pitta bread or crusty rolls.

This recipe is not suitable for freezing.

Borscht

In classic borscht, raw beetroot is used, which is then simmered with beef stock and onion for about 45 minutes. My version uses cooked whole beetroot (not in vinegar) and chicken stock processed together with soured cream. Borscht can be served chilled – the traditional way – or can be heated through and served hot. Either way the colour is stunning.

SERVES 4 TO 6

350 g (12 oz) cooked beetroot, peeled

150 ml (5 fl oz) soured cream or fromage frais

600 ml (1 pint) chicken stock

Snipped fresh chives to garnish

Place the beetroot and half the soured cream or fromage frais in a food processor or blender and process until smooth. Add the chicken stock and process again until smooth. Pour into a bowl and chill well. When completely cold, stir in the remaining soured cream or fromage frais. Serve the soup in individual bowls and garnish with snipped chives.

This recipe is not suitable for freezing.

Smoked Mackerel Pâté

Many savoury pâtés require long slow cooking in a *bain marie*, a water bath, to develop the flavours. This fish pâté is very quick to make using ready-prepared mackerel, especially if you have a blender or a food processor, as it does not require any extra cooking. It will benefit from being well chilled. Try using peppered mackerel, canned tuna or a tin of salmon instead of the smoked mackerel. This pâté makes a very tasty alternative to sandwiches at lunchtime.

SERVES 6

4 × 175 g (6 oz) smoked mackerel fillets, skinned

100 g (4 oz) cream cheese

1 tablespoon horseradish sauce

Finely grated rind and juice of 1 lemon

FOR THE GARNISH

Parsley sprigs

Lemon slices

Place the mackerel, cream cheese, horseradish sauce and lemon rind and juice in a food processor or blender and process until smooth. Turn out into a suitable serving dish, or serve the pâté in individual containers. Garnish with parsley and lemon slices. Serve with hot fingers of toast.

This recipe is not suitable for freezing.

Asparagus with Quick Hollandaise Sauce
⁜

The asparagus season is quite short but as its gets under way the prices do fall, so it's worth taking advantage of it, especially if you can serve it with this delicious short-cut hollandaise sauce. In the traditional version the wine vinegar is first reduced, then the egg yolks are cooked gently in a basin over simmering water until thickened, then finally the butter is whisked in. This sauce cuts out these lengthy processes and is worth a try if you are in a hurry. Allow five or six asparagus spears per person and remember to supply lots of napkins – eating asparagus can be rather a messy business.

SERVES 4

FOR THE HOLLANDAISE SAUCE

2 egg yolks
1 teaspoon white wine vinegar
75 g (3 oz) unsalted butter or
  margarine, melted

Salt and freshly ground
  black pepper

20–24 asparagus spears

Place the egg yolks and wine vinegar in a food processor or blender and process briefly. With the motor running, slowly drizzle in the hot butter or margarine to create a thick creamy sauce. Season with salt and pepper and pour into a warmed serving dish.

The sauce is also very good with 1 tablespoon of chopped fresh parsley, tarragon, basil or snipped fresh chives added to it.

Trim the asparagus spears so that they are all the same length. Remove any of the outer skin which appears hard. Also trim off the V-shaped scales. Rinse, then tie the bundles of asparagus together. So that you do not damage the spears, stand the bundles of asparagus upright in a saucepan, with the heads uppermost. Half-fill the pan with water and cover the asparagus tips with a dome of foil. Bring the water in the pan gently to the boil and simmer for about 8 to 10 minutes. Lift out the asparagus and drain thoroughly. Serve with the hollandaise sauce.

This recipe is not suitable for freezing.

Quick Chicken and Anchovy Soufflé
✤

A traditional hot soufflé is usually made with a thick sauce, to which appropriate flavourings are then added. In my short-cut version I don't use a sauce – I simply rely on the egg yolks and the whisked egg whites folded into the chicken to achieve the lightness.

SERVES 4

15 g (½ oz) butter or margarine	2 eggs, separated
100 g (4 oz) cooked chicken	2 tablespoons single cream
2 large flat mushrooms	Salt and freshly ground
1 tablespoon anchovy essence	black pepper

Pre-heat the oven to gas mark 4, 180°C (350°F) and grease 4 ramekin dishes with the butter or margarine.

Place the chicken, mushrooms and anchovy essence in a food processor or blender and process until thoroughly mixed. Add the egg yolks and cream and process again briefly. Season to taste with salt and pepper. Place the egg whites in a clean grease-free mixing bowl and whisk until they stand in stiff peaks. Fold the egg whites gently through the chicken mixture. Divide between the ramekins, place on a baking sheet and bake in the oven for 15–20 minutes.

If you prefer you could cook the soufflé in a 600 ml (1 pint) soufflé dish. You will need to bake this at a slightly higher temperature, gas mark 6, 200°C (400°F) for 25 to 30 minutes.

This recipe is not suitable for freezing.

Cullen Skink

This is a classic fish and potato soup which is almost a meal in itself. The finnan haddock is normally poached in water first with the onion. The potato is also cooked separately, then mashed. I have adapted this method to by-pass these fiddly processes. All you need to do is place the smoked fish with the diced waxy potato (so it doesn't break up) in the milk and cook everything together. The dominant flavours of the fish will permeate the milk, making the initial poaching unnecessary, and the resulting soup is just as good as the traditionally made variety. Serve with home-made Soda Bread (page 107).

SERVES 4

450 g (1 lb) finnan haddock fillets

25 g (1 oz) unsalted butter or margarine

225 g (8 oz) onions, peeled and finely chopped

900 ml (1½ pints) milk

225 g (8 oz) potatoes, peeled and diced

Freshly ground black pepper

5 tablespoons double cream or fromage frais

Snipped fresh chives to garnish

Cut the haddock into bite-sized chunks. Melt the butter or margarine in a medium saucepan, add the onion and cook until softened without allowing the onion to brown. Gradually add the milk, stirring continuously, then the haddock, followed by the potato. Season to taste with pepper. Bring to the boil then simmer very gently for 12 to 15 minutes, stirring occasionally, until the potato is tender. It is important to keep the heat fairly low or the fish will break up too much. Taste the soup and adjust the seasoning if necessary. Stir in the cream or fromage frais then serve in individual bowls, garnished with snipped chives.

To freeze: do not add the cream or fromage frais. Cool, cover and freeze for up to 2 months.

To defrost: overnight in the fridge then re-heat thoroughly. Stir in the cream or fromage frais before serving.

Creamed Butter Bean Soup

—————— ✤ ——————

Home-made soups normally rely on a robust well made stock for their flavour. The short-cut that most of us rely on is one we probably feel the most guilty about – using stock cubes. If you have time to make stock and freeze it in batches, that's fine. But we don't always have time to fit making stock into our busy routines, so there is no harm in using stock cubes instead. The jars of concentrated vegetable stock are also excellent and tend to be less salty than stock cubes. In this soup I have also used tinned butter beans instead of fresh vegetables – you will probably have the beans in your short-cut store cupboard anyway so you could produce this tasty soup at a moment's notice.

SERVES 4

2 tablespoons vegetable oil
1 onion, peeled and chopped
1 leek, finely chopped
1 medium potato, peeled
  and diced
2 sticks celery, chopped
1 teaspoon paprika
100 g (4 oz) tinned butter
  beans, drained and rinsed
600 ml (1 pint) strong
  chicken stock

600 ml (1 pint) milk
1 bay leaf
150 ml (5 fl oz) single cream
  or fromage frais
Salt and freshly ground
  black pepper
Chopped fresh parsley or
  coriander to garnish

Heat the oil and fry the onion, leek, potato, celery and paprika for about 5 minutes. Add the beans and chicken stock and bring to the boil, stirring occasionally. Reduce the heat, add the milk and bay leaf and simmer gently for 15 to 20 minutes until the beans and vegetables are tender. Remove the bay leaf. Pour the soup into a food processor or blender and process until smooth. Return the soup to the rinsed-out pan. Stir in the cream or fromage frais and season to taste with salt and pepper. Re-heat the soup gently but do not allow it to boil or the cream or fromage frais will separate out. Garnish with chopped fresh parsley or coriander.

To freeze: do not add the cream or fromage frais. Cool, cover and freeze for up to 3 months.
To defrost: overnight in the fridge then re-heat thoroughly. Stir in the cream or fromage frais before serving.

Chicken Pâté

Home-made pâté is totally unlike the bought variety – you cannot beat its wholesome 'bite' – but these pâtés are generally cooked 'long and slow' to develop the flavours, in a bain marie, a water bath. This method is not very practicable because the pâté may then have to be weighted down overnight before it can be served. This short-cut chicken pâté cuts out these processes because the cooking takes place on the hob using quick-to-cook chicken livers so it only takes about 10 minutes.

SERVES 4

50 g (2 oz) butter or margarine
2 tablespoons vegetable oil
1 small onion, peeled and finely chopped
2 cloves garlic, peeled and crushed
450 g (1 lb) chicken livers, trimmed

2 tablespoons orange juice
150 ml (5 fl oz) double cream, low fat double cream or fromage frais
Salt and freshly ground black pepper

FOR THE GARNISH

Lemon slices

Fresh herb sprigs

Heat the butter or margarine with the oil and fry the onion and garlic for 5 minutes until softened and golden brown. Add the chicken livers and cook for 10 to 12 minutes, stirring occasionally. Remove the pan from the heat and stir in the orange juice and cream or fromage frais and season well with salt and pepper. Pour the mixture into a food processor or blender and process until smooth. Taste and adjust the seasoning if necessary. Pour into ramekin dishes, cover and chill the pâté overnight. Serve the pâté garnished with lemon slices and fresh herbs.

This recipe is not suitable for freezing.

Carrot and Orange Soup
⟐

Don't feel guilty about using stock cubes or concentrated stock if you don't have time to make your own – it is a useful short-cut that we all use. Once the stock is combined with the other strongly flavoured ingredients you will not notice the difference. My other short-cut tip is to use a food processor or blender rather than rubbing the soup through a sieve as this will give you a creamy smooth texture.

SERVES 4

25 g (1 oz) butter or margarine
750 g (1½ lb) carrots, sliced
225 g (8 oz) onions, peeled and sliced
1 litre (1¾ pints) chicken or ham stock
Salt and freshly ground black pepper
1 orange

Melt the butter or margarine in a saucepan, add the vegetables and cook gently for 10 minutes until softened slightly. Add the stock and bring to the boil. Lower the heat, cover and simmer for about 25 minutes or until the vegetables are tender.

Meanwhile, pare half the orange rind thinly, using a potato peeler, then cut the rind into shreds. Simmer the shreds in gently boiling water for about 5 minutes until tender. Drain well. Finely grate the remaining orange rind.

Pour the vegetables and half the stock into a food processor or blender and process until smooth. Return this to the stock remaining in the pan. Season to taste with salt and pepper and stir in the grated orange rind. Squeeze the juice of the orange into the pan. Re-heat the soup gently, then taste and adjust the seasoning if necessary. Serve hot, garnished with the shreds of orange rind.

To freeze: cool, cover and freeze for up to 3 months.
To defrost: overnight in the fridge then re-heat thoroughly.

Snacks and Light Meals

It's always a good idea to have a few recipes to hand which are substantial enough to keep the hunger pangs at bay but which are also fast and easy to prepare for lunch or supper.

Quiches and pizzas fit the bill perfectly. To save time I have made use of bought pastry cases for the quiche bases and used a quick scone dough for the pizzas instead of the lengthy yeast dough.

You will find a good selection of frozen ready-to-use pastries in the freezer section of your local supermarket. I have used the very convenient puff pastry sheets for the Savoury Sausage Jalousie (page 35), my short-cut answer to the lengthier process of making sausage rolls.

There are some recipes like the very tasty Dauphinoise (page 29) which can easily be made into a main meal by adding ham or bacon and cheese.

I also find that many pie recipes can be short-cut if you replace the more usual pastry with a crumble topping, as in the Leek, Ham and Mushroom Crumble (page 27). It is even possible to create a substantial short-cut meal from sandwiches by cooking them in a savoury egg custard as in the Savoury Sandwich Pudding (page 26).

Triple Cheese Tart

✣

A well flavoured quiche is a useful recipe to have in your short-cut repertoire. I have saved time in this version by using a pack of frozen shortcrust pastry, or perhaps you might like to try the new frozen rich shortcrust pastry – both these products are available in the freezer section of your local supermarket. If you make quiches regularly you will know that most recipes expect you to bake the pastry shell 'blind' before adding the filling. I find this is unnecessary if you stand your quiche tin on a metal baking sheet which has been warmed as you pre-heat the oven. This helps to transfer the heat through to the pastry and the filling, enabling you to cook the filling and pastry together. If, like me, you hate peeling onions and always end up in tears, I hope you like my easy answer – spring onions.

SERVES 4

50 g (2 oz) Cheddar cheese, grated
50 g (2 oz) Sage Derby cheese, grated
50 g (2 oz) Stilton cheese, grated
2 eggs, beaten
150 ml (5 fl oz) milk or soured cream
4 spring onions, thinly sliced
1 × 18 cm (7 in) ready-made flan case

Place a baking sheet in the oven and pre-heat the oven to gas mark 6, 200°C (400°F).

Mix together the cheeses in a mixing bowl. Stir in the eggs, followed by the milk or soured cream. Finally stir in the spring onions. Stand the pastry case on the baking sheet. Pour the mixture into the pastry case and smooth the filling. Bake in the oven for about 25 minutes until evenly browned and set. Serve with a mixed salad and jacket potatoes.

To freeze: cool, cover and freeze for up to 3 months.
To defrost: 2–3 hours at cool room temperature then re-heat in the oven at gas mark 5, 190°C (375°F) for 15–20 minutes.

Savoury Sandwich Pudding

Sandwiches with interesting fillings provide great snacks for any occasion, but here's a short-cut to turn them into a tasty meal by cooking them in a savoury egg custard. You can combine lots of different sandwich fillings in the same dish and use up left-overs from the fridge to provide the family with a tasty alternative to toasted sandwiches.

Use a mixture of white and brown bread and spread with softened butter, or a low fat alternative. Why not try a selection of the following fillings: chopped cooked chicken with pickle or chutney; cream cheese mixed with finely chopped salami; egg mayonnaise and chopped crisp bacon; tomato and cheese.

SERVES 4

8 slices bread, buttered	450 ml (15 fl oz) milk
Sandwich filling of your choice	2 teaspoons made mustard
75 g (3 oz) Leicester cheese	Salt and freshly ground black pepper
3 eggs	

FOR THE GARNISH

Tomato slices	Parsley sprigs

Pre-heat the oven to gas mark 6, 200°C (400°F).

Use bread to make sandwiches, remove the crusts and cut the sandwiches into triangles. Arrange in a shallow greased 1.2 litre (2 pint) ovenproof dish. Sprinkle with 50 g (2 oz) of the Leicester cheese. Whisk together the eggs, milk, mustard and salt and pepper. Pour this mixture over the bread, pushing the sandwiches gently under the liquid if necessary. Sprinkle with the remaining cheese, leave to soak for 15 minutes if you can, otherwise just bake in the oven for 40 to 45 minutes until the pudding is set, well risen and golden brown. Garnish with tomato slices and parsley and serve piping hot.

This recipe is not suitable for freezing.

Leek, Ham and Mushroom Crumble

—————— ✛ ——————

There is nothing nicer than a leek and ham pie, but making puff pastry is low on the list of priorities if time is at a premium so why not use a crumble topping instead – it provides a tasty alternative to pastry and is very speedily made. Of course, another easy short-cut is to cook individual sheets of ready-rolled frozen pastry and serve them separately – as in my Steak and Kidney Pie (page 82).

SERVES 4

450 g (1 lb) leeks, thinly sliced

40 g (1½ oz) butter or margarine

75 g (3 oz) mushrooms, thinly sliced

25 g (1 oz) plain flour

150 ml (5 fl oz) chicken stock

150 ml (5 fl oz) milk

100 g (4 oz) cooked ham, diced

Salt and freshly ground black pepper

FOR THE CRUMBLE TOPPING

75 g (3 oz) butter or margarine

175 g (6 oz) wholemeal plain flour

25 g (1 oz) sesame seeds

25 g (1 oz) cheese, grated

FOR THE PEANUT AND PARSLEY CRUMBLE TOPPING

100 g (4 oz) unsalted peanuts, coarsely chopped

100 g (4 oz) wholemeal breadcrumbs

A handful of chopped fresh parsley

100 g (4 oz) Cheddar cheese, grated

2 bacon rashers, finely chopped and grilled until crispy

Pre-heat the oven to gas mark 6, 200°C (400°F) and lightly grease a 1.5 litre (2½ pint) pie dish.

Place the leeks and mushrooms in a saucepan with the butter or margarine and cook over a gentle heat, stirring occasionally, until they soften. Do not allow them to brown. Remove the pan from the heat.

27

Whisk the flour, stock and milk together in a jug then pour into the pan with the leeks. Return to the heat and cook the all-in-one sauce, stirring continuously, until it thickens and boils. Add the diced ham and season to taste with salt and pepper. Spoon into the prepared pie dish.

To make the crumble topping, rub the butter or margarine into the flour. Stir in the sesame seeds and grated cheese. Pile the crumble mixture over the leek sauce.

Alternatively, make the peanut topping. Place the peanuts, breadcrumbs, parsley, cheese, and grilled bacon bits in a large mixing bowl. Stir well together then spoon over the leek, ham and mushroom filling.

Bake in the oven for 25 to 30 minutes until the crumble topping is golden brown.

To freeze: assemble the crumble but do not bake. Cool, cover and freeze for up to 3 months.

To defrost: overnight in the fridge then re-heat at gas mark 4, 180°C (350°F) for 25–30 minutes. Cover with foil if the crumble begins to brown too much.

Cheesey Meringue

This is an alternative filling to the usual custard base found in a quiche. It is basically an all-in-one sauce spooned into a ready-made flan case and topped with a cheesey meringue. Although it does need to go into the oven, the total cooking time is much shorter than usual so it's a good recipe if you want a quiche in a hurry. Pre-heating the baking sheet will help the pastry to cook more quickly too.

SERVES 4

25 g (1 oz) butter or polyunsaturated margarine
175 g (6 oz) mushrooms, sliced
25 g (1 oz) plain flour
300 ml (10 fl oz) milk
2 egg yolks, beaten
50 g (2 oz) Cheddar cheese, grated
1 × 18 cm (7 in) ready-made flan case

FOR THE TOPPING

2 egg whites
A pinch of salt
50 g (2 oz) Cheddar or
   Leicester cheese, grated

Paprika

Place a baking sheet in the oven and pre-heat the oven to gas mark 6, 200°C (400°F).

Melt the butter or margarine in a saucepan, add the mushrooms and cook gently until golden brown. Remove the pan from the heat and cool slightly. Whisk the flour and milk together in a basin, then pour into the pan. Return to the heat and gradually bring to the boil, whisking continuously until the sauce has thickened. Remove from the heat and beat in the egg yolks and grated cheese. Simmer over a medium heat, stirring continuously, until the cheese and egg are thoroughly incorporated into the sauce. Place the flan case on the baking sheet and pour in the cheese sauce.

Place the egg whites in a large grease-free mixing bowl. Whisk until the egg whites stand in stiff peaks. Fold in the grated cheese and salt. Pile the cheesey meringue on top of the cheese sauce. Dust with paprika. Bake in the oven for 15 to 20 minutes until the meringue is lightly browned. Serve with a mixed green salad and French Dressing (page 122).

This recipe is not suitable for freezing.

Bacon Dauphinoise

A dauphinoise is a delicious gratin usually made with potato and onion only. You can have a short-cut to a complete meal by adding chopped bacon or ham and some extra cheese. The dauphinoise then makes a delicious one-pot lunch or supper dish for the family. You can use a food processor to slice the onions and potatoes quickly.

SERVES 4

225 g (8 oz) bacon or ham, rinded and diced

3 tablespoons olive oil

450 g (1 lb) onions, peeled and thinly sliced

2 cloves garlic, peeled and crushed

1 tablespoon brown sugar

900 g (2 lb) old potatoes, peeled and thinly sliced

Salt and freshly ground black pepper

175 g (6 oz) Cheddar cheese, grated

1 egg

150 ml (5 fl oz) milk

150 ml (5 fl oz) soured cream or use all milk

A pinch of freshly grated nutmeg

Pre-heat the oven to gas mark 5, 190°C (375°F) and grease a 2 litre (3½ pint) shallow ovenproof dish.

Place the diced bacon in a non-stick frying pan and fry for about 5 minutes, adding a little oil if necessary. Remove from the pan with a slotted spoon and drain on kitchen paper. Pour the oil into the pan and heat gently then fry the onions, garlic and sugar over a medium heat, stirring frequently, until the onions begin to soften.

Cover the bottom of the prepared dish with a layer of potatoes and season lightly with salt and pepper. Add a layer of onions, then the bacon and some of the cheese, seasoning as you go. Continue layering the potatoes, onions, bacon and cheese, finishing with a layer of potatoes.

Beat together the egg, milk and soured cream. Heat gently to blood temperature. Pour over the potato mixture in the dish, pushing the potatoes down to keep them covered. If you think you need more milk, add it at this stage. Place the dish on a baking sheet and sprinkle with nutmeg. Cook in the oven for 45 to 55 minutes until golden brown. Serve piping hot with hunks of crusty, warm French bread.

To freeze: cool, cover and freeze for up to 3 months.
To defrost: overnight in the refrigerator then re-heat thoroughly covered with a sheet of foil.

Cheese and Onion Quiche

There's no need to feel guilty about using ready-made flan cases as quiche bases – when you are short of time pastry-making is just too time-consuming. I have also speeded up the preparation of the filling by using spring onion, which you won't have to pre-cook like ordinary onions. The final trick is to use yoghurt and egg instead of the usual milk-based mixture. The yoghurt mixture is thicker and tends to set more quickly than the normal custard.

SERVES 4

2 eggs
150 ml (5 fl oz) natural
  yoghurt or milk
Salt and freshly ground
  black pepper
100 g (4 oz) Cheddar cheese,
  grated

1 bunch spring onions,
  finely chopped
1 teaspoon English mustard
  (or to taste)
1 × 18 cm (7 in) ready-made
  flan case

Place a baking sheet in the oven and pre-heat the oven to gas mark 5, 190°C (375°F).

In a basin, beat together the eggs and yoghurt and season with salt and pepper. Stir in the grated cheese, mixing well, followed by the spring onions and mustard. Place the flan case on the baking sheet, pour in the egg custard and smooth the top.

Bake in the oven for about 20 minutes until the egg mixture is set and light golden brown in colour. The flan is delicious either eaten on its own or with jacket potatoes, or a new potato salad in the summer.

To freeze: cool, cover and freeze for up to 3 months.
To defrost: 2–3 hours at cool room temperature then re-heat in the oven at gas mark 5, 190°C (375°F) for 15–20 minutes.

Frying Pan Pizza

This is one occasion when you need not feel guilty about getting out the frying pan. I have by-passed the time-consuming traditional yeast-based dough in favour of this pizza which is cooked in a frying pan and not in the oven. Using this method will save you even more time, and you can even serve the pizza straight from the pan on to individual plates. You can add almost anything you like to make a variety of different toppings.

SERVES 4

225 g (8 oz) self-raising flour
Salt and freshly ground
   black pepper
4 tablespoons vegetable oil
4 tablespoons cold water
5 tablespoons tomato purée
1 × 400 g (14 oz) tin chopped
   tomatoes with herbs,
   drained

175 g (6 oz) Red Leicester
   cheese, grated
½ teaspoon dried oregano
A few black olives to garnish
   (optional)

Place the flour and seasoning in a mixing bowl. Make a well in the centre of the flour and pour in 2 tablespoons of the oil and the 4 tablespoons of cold water. Using a round-bladed knife, mix to a soft but not sticky dough. Depending on the absorbency of the flour you may need to add a little more water. Turn the dough on to a floured surface and roll or pat the mixture to a circle large enough to fit a medium-sized frying pan, about 20 cm (8 in).

Heat the remaining 2 tablespoons of oil in the frying pan. Add the dough and cook gently until the base is lightly browned. Flip the pizza base on to a plate, uncooked side uppermost. If necessary place a little more oil in the pan. Slide the dough back into the pan, this time with the browned side uppermost. Spread with the tomato purée, chopped tomatoes and cheese. Sprinkle with oregano and top with the olives, if using. Return the pan to the heat and cook for a further 5 minutes until the dough is fully cooked through.

Pre-heat the grill, and cook the top of the pizza until the cheese is bubbling and lightly browned. Cut into wedges and serve whilst piping hot. This is delicious served with a mixed salad.

This recipe is not suitable for freezing.

Wholemeal Pizza

A light, crumbly scone-based dough made with wholemeal flour is perfect for this pizza and you will also save yourself the kneading, rising and proving demanded by the usual pizza base.

SERVES 4

50 g (2 oz) butter or margarine

225 g (8 oz) wholemeal self-raising flour

A pinch of salt

150 ml (5 fl oz) milk

1½ tablespoons vegetable oil

2 medium onions, peeled and chopped

1 × 400 g (14 oz) tin chopped tomatoes with herbs, drained

1–2 cloves garlic, peeled and crushed

1 teaspoon dried oregano

Salt and freshly ground black pepper

100 g (4 oz) cooked ham, chopped

75 g (3 oz) Red Leicester cheese, grated

A few black olives (optional)

2 rashers bacon, rinded and cut into long strips

Pre-heat the oven to gas mark 6, 200°C (400°F) and lightly grease a baking sheet.

Place the butter or margarine, flour and salt in a large mixing bowl. Rub the fat into the flour until it resembles breadcrumbs. Add sufficient milk to mix to a soft but not sticky dough. Turn the dough on to a floured board, pat into a round with the palm of the hand then roll lightly with a rolling pin into a circle about 20 cm (8 in) round. Brush with a little vegetable oil and lift on to the baking sheet.

Meanwhile heat the remaining oil in a medium saucepan, add the onions, tomatoes, garlic and oregano, stir well and bring to the boil.

Simmer gently for about 10 minutes until most of the tomato liquid has evaporated. Season to taste with salt and pepper. Leave to cool.

Spoon the cooled filling on to the pizza base. Sprinkle the ham over the filling, scatter with the grated cheese and a few black olives, if using. Arrange the bacon strips in a criss-cross pattern over the pizza. Bake in the oven for about 25 minutes until the base is cooked through and the topping is bubbling and golden brown. Serve with a green salad and French Dressing made with a crushed clove of garlic (page 122).

This recipe is not suitable for freezing.

Roly-Poly Pizza

❖

This is my short-cut version of the traditional calzone pizza – the classic Italian creation where the filling is enclosed within the dough. Again my simple scone dough comes in very handy rolled around a savoury filling of tomato, bacon and cheese. For children and teenagers who never get tired of pizza, this could be an interesting alternative.

SERVES 4

225 g (8 oz) self-raising flour   150 ml (5 fl oz) milk
50 g (2 oz) butter or margarine

FOR THE FILLING

3 rashers middle bacon or ham, rinded and diced

1 × 200 g (7 oz) tin chopped tomatoes

1½ tablespoons coarse-grain mustard

150 g (5 oz) well-flavoured cheese, grated

½ teaspoon paprika

1 egg, beaten

Pre-heat the oven to gas mark 6, 200°C (400°F), and lightly grease a baking sheet.

Place the flour and butter or margarine in a mixing bowl and rub the fat into the flour until the mixture resembles breadcrumbs. Add sufficient milk to mix to a soft but not sticky dough. Turn the dough on to a floured board and roll to a 30 × 25 cm (12 × 10 in) rectangle. Cover with a tea towel.

Meanwhile prepare the filling. Place the diced bacon or ham in a saucepan with the tomatoes and cook together until most of the tomato liquid has evaporated. Leave to cool. Spread the mustard over the rolled-out dough, leaving a 1 cm (½ in) border. Top with the tomatoes, sprinkle with grated cheese then dust with paprika. Starting at the longest edge of the dough, roll up Swiss roll fashion to enclose the filling. Place, seam side down, on the baking sheet. Brush lightly with beaten egg. Bake in the oven for about 20 to 25 minutes until golden brown. Serve piping hot.

VARIATIONS

Try substituting pepperoni for the bacon or ham. Use tomato purée instead of mustard, or add a tablespoon of chopped olives and a teaspoon of dried basil, or you can create your own filling from the short-cut store cupboard.

To freeze: cool, cover and freeze for up to 2 months.
To defrost: overnight in the fridge then re-heat thoroughly.

Savoury Sausage Jalousie

This is my alternative to sausage rolls: a tasty onion and sausage mixture sandwiched between sheets of ready-rolled pastry. It saves on all that rolling, shaping and cutting when making individual sausage rolls. Just cut the jalousie into individual portions when baked and serve with crunchy coleslaw and a salad.

SERVES 4

2 sheets frozen ready-rolled
  puff pastry
275 g (10 oz) pork sausage
  meat
1 medium onion, peeled and
  grated

2 teaspoons tomato purée
½ teaspoon dried mixed
  herbs
1 egg, beaten

Pre-heat the oven to gas mark 6, 200°C (400°F) and lightly grease a baking sheet.

Place one sheet of pastry on the baking sheet. Prick the surface lightly with a fork, taking care not to go through to the base. Place the sausage meat in a mixing bowl, add the onion, tomato purée and mixed herbs and mix well together, breaking up the sausage meat. Spread the sausage mixture over the pastry, leaving a gap of about 1 cm (½ in) all round. Brush the edges of the pastry with beaten egg and place the second sheet of pastry on top. Press the pastry edges together then flute them with your thumb and forefinger, or just press all round with a fork to seal the edges together. Brush the surface of the pastry with beaten egg and make 2 or 3 slits with a pair of scissors to release any steam. Bake in the oven for 25 to 30 minutes until the pastry is well risen and golden brown. Serve as a light supper dish or cut into slices as a snack, or pop a portion into lunch boxes.

This recipe is not suitable for freezing.

Vegetable Dishes

The preparation and cooking of interesting vegetable dishes can be a lengthy process and no one wants to eat just plain sliced and boiled vegetables all the time. But there are several ways you can short-cut this to provide nourishing healthy dishes for the family.

One of my favourite tips is to cook a selection of vegetables together. Why not try the Supper Party Vegetables (page 41) – a selection of seasonal vegetables steamed together in a greaseproof paper bag.

Filo pastry is a great alternative to all the rolling out required with frozen puff pastry, and it makes a crunchy topping for vegetable pies. If the vegetables are cooked together, the result is an excellent combination of flavours.

I have also used tinned beans to create a risotto (page 38) and a goulash (page 44) – both traditionally made with meat, which takes longer to cook. Canned beans need no soaking or pre-cooking, heat through quickly and are full of fibre and protein to provide a quick but nourishing meal for a vegetarian or a meat lover.

Aduki Bean Risotto

In my version, the classic Italian risotto becomes a main course meal with the addition of tinned aduki beans and the liquid is added all in one go, instead of in stages as is done with traditional risottos. There's plenty of flavour and colour with the paprika and peppers. Arborio rice is favoured by the Italians for its distinctive flavour and texture, but ordinary long-grain rice will work. Mop up the juices with Italian ciabatta bread or the lovely olive bread you can buy in delicatessens or supermarkets.

SERVES 4

- 1–2 tablespoons olive oil
- 1 large onion, peeled and chopped
- 1–2 cloves garlic, peeled and crushed
- 1 red chilli pepper, de-seeded and chopped
- 1 red pepper, de-seeded and diced
- ½ teaspoon paprika
- ½ teaspoon ground coriander
- 225 g (8 oz) Arborio rice
- 450 ml (15 fl oz) vegetable stock
- 1 × 400 g (14 oz) tin chopped tomatoes
- 1 × 300 g (11 oz) tin aduki beans, drained and rinsed
- 1 bay leaf
- Salt and freshly ground black pepper

Heat the oil in a large frying pan and gently fry the onion, garlic, chilli pepper and pepper until soft but not brown. Add the paprika and coriander and cook for 1 minute, stirring constantly. Add the rice, stock, tomatoes, aduki beans and bay leaf. Stir well to mix the ingredients together. Bring to the boil, then reduce the heat, cover and simmer gently for 20 minutes or until the rice is cooked through. Most of the liquid should have been absorbed. Check and adjust the seasoning to taste. Serve whilst piping hot, with warmed ciabatta bread or olive bread.

This recipe is not suitable for freezing.

Spicy Cauliflower with Coriander

———————— ✛ ————————

I love to serve a selection of different vegetables at family meals and for entertaining – but it's often difficult to find room for all the pans and dishes. This spicy cauliflower is my short-cut answer – an assortment of different vegetables cooked together in a spicy stock. The result is one, I'm sure, you'll want to repeat often. It can become the base for a savoury crumble or a pie if you choose one of the alternative toppings used for Filo-Topped Vegetable Pie (page 42) or Crunchy Vegetable Crumble (page 43).

SERVES 4

2 tablespoons vegetable oil
1 teaspoon ground ginger
2 teaspoons ground coriander
1 teaspoon turmeric
2 sticks celery, sliced
1 onion, peeled and sliced

2 carrots, sliced
1 cauliflower, broken into florets
120 ml (4 fl oz) vegetable stock
150 ml (5 fl oz) natural yoghurt

FOR THE GARNISH

Chopped fresh parsley   Chopped fresh coriander

Heat the oil in a medium saucepan. Add the spices and cook over a low heat for 2 to 3 minutes to release the flavours. Add the celery, onion, carrots and cauliflower. Stir the vegetables around in the spices to coat fully, then stir in the stock. Cover with a tightly-fitting lid and cook the vegetables for about 10 to 15 minutes until they are softened, but still *al dente*. Drain any excess liquid from the vegetables. Serve in a shallow dish with the yoghurt spooned over the top. Garnish with the parsley and coriander.

This recipe is not suitable for freezing.

Mushroom Stroganoff

Here's a tasty short-cut if you find yourself short of meat. A traditional stroganoff is made using strips of rump steak. Just substitute mushrooms instead to make this tasty version. The mushrooms are like little sponges, absorbing all the flavours from the sauce. You can, of course, add extra fibre and protein in the form of tinned beans. Serve the dish with nutty wholegrain rice.

SERVES 4

3 tablespoons vegetable oil
1 onion, peeled and sliced
275 g (10 oz) flat
   mushrooms, sliced
1 red pepper, de-seeded and
   sliced
1 green pepper, de-seeded
   and sliced
225 g (8 oz) button
   mushrooms, sliced
2 tablespoons plain flour

350 ml (12 fl oz) vegetable
   stock
2 tablespoons Worcestershire
   sauce
4 teaspoons horseradish
   sauce
Salt and freshly ground
   black pepper
3 tablespoons single cream
   or fromage frais

Heat the oil and cook the onion and large mushrooms over a gentle heat until softened. Do not allow them to brown. Stir in the remaining vegetables and cook for about 3 minutes. Remove from the heat and stir in the flour then return to the heat and cook for about 1 minute. Gradually stir in the stock and bring to the boil, stirring constantly. Stir in the Worcestershire sauce and horseradish sauce and season with salt and pepper. Simmer for about 15 minutes, stirring from time to time. Remove from the heat and stir in the cream or fromage frais. Return the goulash to the heat and heat through gently but do not allow to boil.

To freeze: do not add the cream or fromage frais. Cool, cover and freeze for up to 3 months.
To defrost: overnight in the fridge then re-heat thoroughly adding the cream or fromage frais as described above.

Supper Party Vegetables

❖

This recipe was given to me by a friend who had just moved house. Her kitchen was upside down, but this was her answer to cooking the vegetables – she just popped them all in a greaseproof paper bag and steamed them. The all-in-one sauce adds a tasty finishing touch. You will need four greaseproof paper bags.

SERVES 4

175 g (6 oz) Brussels sprouts
175 g (6 oz) carrots, sliced
175 g (6 oz) cauliflower, broken into florets
175 g (6 oz) swede, peeled and diced
2 sticks celery, sliced
Salt and freshly ground black pepper

1 tablespoon dried mixed herbs
15 g (½ oz) plain flour
250 ml (8 fl oz) milk
15 g (½ oz) butter or margarine
3 tablespoons white wine (optional)
2 tablespoons chopped fresh parsley

Prepare all the vegetables and ensure that they are all roughly of a similar size when sliced or diced – this will help them to cook in the same length of time. Season with salt and pepper and toss in the mixed herbs. Place them in the bags and seal the parcels well to retain the moisture. Place them in a large colander or steamer over a pan of gently simmering water. Steam for about 20 minutes.

Meanwhile make the sauce. Whisk the flour into the milk then dot in the butter or margarine. Gradually bring the sauce to the boil, stirring constantly until the sauce has thickened. Stir in the wine, if using.

When the vegetables are cooked, empty the paper parcels on to individual plates, spoon over the sauce and sprinkle with the parsley.

This recipe is not suitable for freezing.

Filo-Topped Vegetable Pie

❖

If I want a short-cut pastry topping and one which is a bit lighter than the usual flaky or puff varieties, I always use filo pastry. It can be bought in packets from the freezer section of your local supermarket. The packs consist of thin sheets of pastry which you can brush with oil or melted butter or margarine and then layer up to give a crisp topping. I find 4 or 5 sheets are enough for this pie. The filling is delicious, too – a whole variety of different vegetables – but you only need one pan to cook them in – a real short-cut tip.

SERVES 4

1 tablespoon vegetable oil
1 onion, peeled and chopped
2 carrots, finely chopped
450 g (1 lb) courgettes, diced
100 g (4 oz) mushrooms, sliced
2 medium tomatoes, skinned and chopped
½ teaspoon dried thyme
½ teaspoon dried marjoram
2 tablespoons chopped fresh parsley

2 tablespoons tomato purée
2 tablespoons dark soy sauce
Salt and freshly ground black pepper
4 sheets filo pastry
50 g (2 oz) margarine, melted
1 egg, beaten
1 tablespoon sesame seeds

Pre-heat the oven to gas mark 6, 200°C (400°F) and lightly grease a rectangular ovenproof dish.

Heat the oil in a saucepan and cook the onion until soft. Add the carrots, courgettes, mushrooms and tomatoes then the herbs. Mix all the vegetables well, then cover with a lid and cook for 10 to 15 minutes until the vegetables are soft but not squashy. Add the tomato purée and soy sauce and season with salt and pepper. Spread the vegetables out on a plate and leave to cool. When the mixture has cooled, spoon into the ovenproof dish.

Take one sheet of filo pastry and brush with melted margarine. Take a second sheet of pastry and place over the first sheet, brush as before with melted margarine. Continue layering up the pastry, brushing each sheet as you go. Lift the sheets of filo pastry and place them over the vegetables. Press the pastry down gently, then cut off any excess from the edges. Brush with beaten egg and sprinkle with sesame seeds. Bake in the oven for 15 to 20 minutes until the pastry is golden brown and crisp. Serve with minted new potatoes.

This recipe is not suitable for freezing.

Crunchy Vegetable Crumble

Here's one of my favourite time-saving tips for those occasions when I want to serve several vegetables together at a particular meal – I turn them into a crumble. The vegetables are all steamed together first, before being smothered with an all-in-one sauce then topped off with a crunchy crumble.

SERVES 4

350 g (12 oz) broccoli florets
225 g (8 oz) carrots, diced
1 leek, sliced
1 red pepper, de-seeded and diced
25 g (1 oz) wholemeal plain flour

450 ml (15 fl oz) milk
40 g (1½ oz) butter or margarine
2 teaspoons creamed horseradish
1 × 400 g (14 oz) tin butter beans, drained and rinsed

FOR THE CRUMBLE TOPPING

50 g (2 oz) polyunsaturated margarine
100 g (4 oz) wholemeal plain flour

25 g (1 oz) rolled oats
1 tablespoon sesame seeds
75 g (3 oz) vegetarian Cheddar cheese, grated

Pre-heat the oven to gas mark 6, 200°C (400°F).

Steam the broccoli, carrots, leek and pepper for 8 to 10 minutes or until they are cooked through, but take care not to overcook – they should still remain a little crunchy.

Meanwhile make the sauce. Whisk the flour into the milk. Dot with butter or margarine. Bring the sauce to the boil, whisking continuously until the sauce thickens. Stir in the horseradish. Place the steamed vegetables in a large ovenproof casserole dish and add the butter beans, mixing briefly. Pour the sauce over the vegetables, making sure that they are all covered.

To make the crumble topping, rub the margarine into the flour then stir in the oats and sesame seeds and finally the grated cheese. Pile the crumble mixture over the vegetables. Bake in the oven for 25 to 30 minutes until bubbling and golden brown. Serve as a lunch or supper dish with crusty brown rolls and a crisp green salad.

To freeze: cool, cover and freeze for up to 3 months.
To defrost: overnight in the fridge then re-heat at gas mark 6, 200°C (400°F) for 15–20 minutes. Cover with foil if the crumble begins to brown too much.

Mixed Bean Goulash

The traditional meat-based goulash involves soaking and pre-cooking beans and a long cooking time. My version uses tinned beans which, of course, don't need to be soaked. The three types of beans, combined with the delicious tang of tomato, create a good balance of flavour and texture – and I promise you won't notice the lack of meat. This is the perfect dish if you are entertaining vegetarian and non-vegetarian friends as we often do.

SERVES 4

2 tablespoons vegetable oil
2 medium onions, peeled and sliced
1 tablespoon paprika
1 × 400 g (14 oz) tin chopped tomatoes with herbs
2 tablespoons tomato purée
300 ml (10 fl oz) beef stock
1 × 425 g (15 oz) tin butter beans, drained and rinsed

1 × 425 g (15 oz) tin red kidney beans, drained and rinsed
1 × 425 g (15 oz) tin borlotti beans, drained and rinsed
150 ml (5 fl oz) natural yoghurt
2 tablespoons finely chopped fresh parsley

Heat the oil in a large saucepan and fry the onions for 5 to 10 minutes until soft but not brown. Stir in the paprika and cook gently for 1 minute. Add the tomatoes, tomato purée, stock and beans. Cover and simmer for 15 to 20 minutes until the sauce has thickened slightly. Spoon the bean goulash into a casserole dish and drizzle with the yoghurt. Sprinkle with the chopped parsley and serve piping hot.

This recipe is not suitable for freezing.

Tasty Bean Bake

You will almost certainly have all the ingredients for this recipe in your store cupboard. Tinned beans avoid the need for soaking, and pre-cooking. Worcestershire and tabasco sauce spice up the beans and the crispy crumble topping turns the dish into a substantial supper-time dish.

SERVES 4

1 tablespoon olive oil

1 large onion, peeled and finely chopped

2 cloves garlic, peeled and crushed

1 teaspoon chilli powder

1 × 400 g (14 oz) tin chopped tomatoes

1 tablespoon tomato purée

A few drops of tabasco sauce

2 tablespoons Worcestershire sauce

1 × 425 g (15 oz) tin cannellini beans, drained and rinsed

1 × 300 g (11 oz) tin red kidney beans, drained and rinsed

1 × 300 g (11 oz) tin butter beans, drained and rinsed

Salt and freshly ground black pepper

FOR THE CRISPY TOPPING

100 g (4 oz) fresh brown breadcrumbs

50 g (2 oz) mature Cheddar cheese, grated

25 g (1 oz) sunflower seeds

25 g (1 oz) chopped fresh parsley

Pre-heat the oven to gas mark 6, 200°C (400°F).

Heat the oil in a flameproof casserole or large frying pan. Add the onion and garlic and cook for about 5 minutes until softened but not coloured. Add the chilli powder and cook gently for 2 minutes to release the flavour. Stir in the tomatoes, tomato purée, tabasco sauce and Worcestershire sauce. Next stir in the beans and season well with salt and pepper. Bring to the boil then simmer for 3 to 4 minutes. Taste and adjust the seasoning if necessary. Spoon into a casserole dish.

Mix together the topping ingredients and spoon this mixture over the spicy beans. Bake, uncovered, for about 20 minutes until the crumble topping is golden brown.

This recipe is not suitable for freezing.

Fish Dishes

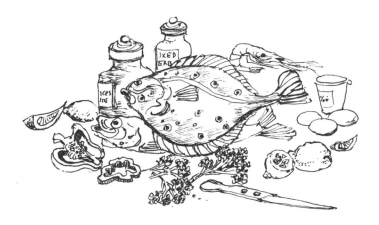

Although we are a nation of fish and chip lovers, fresh fish is still low on most of our shopping lists, and yet it is a very healthy, nourishing and easy-to-prepare food. The traditional fishmonger is more of a rarity these days but most of our major supermarkets have an excellent fish counter. The staff will offer advice on the preparation and cooking of even the most unusual varieties of fish, and the messy business of cleaning and gutting the fish is all taken care of, too.

However, if fish supplies are affected by the weather, there is always a good selection of frozen fish in the supermarket freezer cabinet. The flavour and quality of fish is not affected by the freezing process and the other bonus is that it is very often cheaper than fresh fish, making frozen fish an excellent choice.

Fish is naturally very quick and easy to cook, but there are several ways to short-cut some tasty fish recipes. Traditionally fish is often accompanied by a sauce, but you can by-pass all the usual stirring of a milk-based sauce by using yoghurt. Yoghurt has just the right consistency for a sauce, and can be combined with spices, herbs, cheese, egg, mustard and other ingredients to create a variety of flavours. The yoghurt-based sauce is especially good used in the Haddock Lasagne (page 49).

Many fish recipes suggest steaming the fish first before continuing with the next stage. I find this unnecessary, as you will see in the Catch of the Day Casserole (page 52). Just pop the fish into the casserole dish raw, and add the all-in-one sauce. Other short-cuts include using frozen pastry, as in the Koulibiac (page 54) and making one large fish cake in a pan, to cut out the fiddly shaping of individual fish cakes.

Speedy Sardines

—————— ✥ ——————

Fresh sardines have a unique taste, not at all like their tinned cousins, and they are very economical as well. Cooking fish in individual parcels complete with accompanying vegetables is a real short-cut alternative to steaming or poaching. All the juices remain intact, and the parcels can be served straight on to individual plates – giving the biggest bonus of all as you can certainly cut down on the washing up. You will need either greaseproof paper bags, or squares of parchment paper or greaseproof paper. Foil will also work well.

SERVES 4

1 tablespoon vegetable oil	2 tablespoons chopped fresh
16 fresh sardines	herbs such as parsley, dill,
Salt and freshly ground	chives
black pepper	1 medium courgette, sliced
Juice of 1 lemon or lime	2 medium tomatoes, sliced

Pre-heat the oven to gas mark 5, 190°C (375°F).

Brush the paper or foil with the oil and place 4 sardines on or in each parcel. Season with salt and pepper. Drizzle with lemon or lime juice and scatter with the fresh herbs. Arrange the slices of courgette on top, followed by the sliced tomatoes. Season with salt and pepper. Seal the parcels to keep all the juices and flavours intact. Place the parcels in a baking dish and bake for 20 to 25 minutes until the sardines and vegetables are cooked through. Serve the parcels directly on to individual plates with new potatoes tossed in chopped fresh mint.

This recipe is not suitable for freezing.

Haddock Lasagne

❖

The pre-cooked sheets of lasagne come into their own here because they don't need blanching in boiling water before use, like the conventional variety. You don't need to make a traditional sauce either. I often use the short-cut version, consisting of natural yoghurt and beaten egg enriched with grated cheese. This tasty sauce adds moisture to the savoury lasagne. You can even use frozen fish in this recipe – use it straight from the freezer, breaking it up before using.

SERVES 4

1 tablespoon vegetable oil
1 medium onion, peeled and chopped
100 g (4 oz) button mushrooms
1 × 400 g (14 oz) tin chopped tomatoes
1 tablespoon tomato purée

1 tablespoon chopped fresh parsley
½ teaspoon dried oregano
Salt and freshly ground black pepper
450 g (1 lb) haddock or cod, flaked
6 sheets easy-cook lasagne

FOR THE TOPPING

300 ml (10 fl oz) natural yoghurt
75 g (3 oz) Cheddar cheese, grated

1 egg, beaten
25 g (1 oz) fresh breadcrumbs
Whole prawns to garnish (optional)

Pre-heat the oven to gas mark 5, 190°C (375°F) and grease a large ovenproof dish.

Heat the oil in a saucepan and fry the onion until softened. Stir in the mushrooms, tomatoes, tomato purée, parsley and oregano and season with salt and pepper. Bring to the boil and simmer for 5 minutes. Stir in the flaked fish.

Cover the base of the ovenproof dish with a layer of lasagne sheets, cutting it to fit if necessary. Top the lasagne with half the fish mixture. Repeat the layers until you have used up all the mixture, finishing with a layer of lasagne.

Mix together the yoghurt and 50 g (2 oz) of the cheese, then mix in the beaten egg. Pour this mixture over the layered lasagne. Mix together the remaining cheese with the breadcrumbs. Sprinkle this mixture over the sauce. Bake in the oven for 35 to 40 minutes until the lasagne is bubbling and brown. Garnish with prawns if using, and serve with jacket potatoes and courgettes.

This recipe is not suitable for freezing.

All-in-one Provençal Plaice

This is my short-cut version of the classic Sauce Provençal, the flavour of which is usually obtained by a reduction of the principal ingredients to achieve its unique flavour. My sauce uses a tangy mixture of chopped tinned tomatoes, paprika and tomato purée, baked with the fish to ensure that the flavours are absorbed. Chill a bottle of suitable wine and you can just about imagine you're dining in Provence.

SERVES 4

4 × 150 g (5 oz) pieces of cod, haddock or coley

2 medium onions, peeled and finely chopped

3–4 medium courgettes, sliced

1 red or yellow pepper, de-seeded and diced

1 × 400 g (14 oz) tin chopped tomatoes with herbs

1 tablespoon tomato purée

1 teaspoon paprika

Salt and freshly ground black pepper

Pre-heat the oven to gas mark 4, 180°C (350°F) and lightly grease a shallow ovenproof dish.

Place the portions of fish in the dish. Sprinkle with the onion, then the courgettes and finally the pepper. Mix the chopped tomatoes with the paprika and the tomato purée and pour over the fish and vegetables. Season with salt and pepper. Cover with foil and bake in the oven for 25 to 30 minutes until the fish is cooked through and the sauce is piping hot. When the fish is cooked you will see a white milky fluid between the flakes. Be careful not to overcook the fish or it will be tough and dry. Serve with wholegrain rice and sweetcorn.

This recipe is not suitable for freezing.

Plaice in Yoghurt and Coriander Sauce

Fish always benefits from the addition of a creamy sauce. The classic fish sauces rely on a white sauce made with butter, cornflour or flour and milk or stock. I find that yoghurt is an excellent quicker alternative, and you can add numerous different spices or flavourings to create the taste you want. The yoghurt is naturally thicker than milk or stock so does not require any extra thickening.

SERVES 4

3 tablespoons chopped fresh mint	2 teaspoons paprika
2 cloves garlic, peeled and crushed	Salt and freshly ground black pepper
1 small onion, peeled and chopped	4 plaice fillets
150 ml (5 fl oz) natural yoghurt	75 g (3 oz) butter or margarine, softened
2 teaspoons vegetable oil	1 tablespoon chopped fresh coriander
	Lemon wedges to garnish

Pre-heat the oven to gas mark 4, 180°C (350°F) and lightly grease a shallow ovenproof dish.

Place the mint, garlic, onion, yoghurt, oil, paprika, salt and pepper in a food processor or blender and process until you have a smooth paste. Place the fish in the dish and spread generously with the spiced yoghurt. Cover with a sheet of foil and bake in the oven for 20 to 25 minutes.

Meanwhile mix together the butter or margarine and coriander. Place in the freezer section of the fridge to harden.

When the plaice is cooked, dot with little pats of coriander butter.

Garnish with lemon wedges and serve with new potatoes, broccoli and cauliflower.

This recipe is not suitable for freezing.

Catch of the Day Casserole

I have adapted this particular recipe to include the very versatile all-in-one sauce instead of the usual béchamel sauce and it has proved to be very popular with the members of my men's cookery class. Instead of poaching the fish, I just pop it straight into the casserole dish and cover with the sauce. I find it cooks beautifully and remains moist and succulent. This recipe also makes a good base for a fish pie (page 53).

SERVES 4

450 g (1 lb) haddock, or cod fillet, skinned
225 g (8 oz) smoked haddock
100 g (4 oz) peeled prawns (optional)
1 × 300 g (11 oz) tin sweetcorn kernels, drained
40 g (1½ oz) plain flour
300 ml (10 fl oz) milk, cider or white wine
40 g (1½ oz) butter or margarine, flaked
1 teaspoon made mustard or anchovy essence
1 tablespoon lemon juice
4 tablespoons soured cream
Salt and freshly ground black pepper

Pre-heat the oven to gas mark 4, 180°C (350°F) and lightly grease a shallow ovenproof dish.

Cut the fish into 2.5 cm (1 in cubes). Place in the dish with the prawns and sweetcorn.

To make the sauce, place the flour in a saucepan, whisk in the milk and add the butter in flakes. Bring to the boil, stirring continuously. Stir in the mustard or anchovy essence and lemon juice, followed by the soured cream. Season with salt and pepper and pour the sauce over the fish, prawns and sweetcorn. Cover with foil and bake in the oven for 30 to 35 minutes until the fish is cooked through.

This recipe is not suitable for freezing.

Crunchy Crumble Fish Pie

The previous recipe can become the base for a fish pie but when time is short, peeling and boiling potatoes is not easy, so why not make a crunchy crumble topping using the following recipe or the Peanut and Parsley Crumble (page 27).

SERVES 4

1 quantity Catch of the Day Casserole (page 52)	100 g (4 oz) Cheddar cheese, grated
100 g (4 oz) chopped mixed nuts	1 tablespoon chopped fresh parsley or ½ tablespoon freeze-dried parsley
100 g (4 oz) oatmeal	

Pre-heat the oven to gas mark 5, 190°C (375°F).

Make up the fish casserole following the recipe on page 52.

Place the chopped mixed nuts, oatmeal and grated cheese in a mixing bowl. Stir together, then fold in the parsley. Spoon the crunchy crumble over the fish in its sauce. Smooth out gently but do not press down. Bake in the oven for 30 to 35 minutes until the fish is cooked and the crumble topping is golden brown.

This recipe is not suitable for freezing.

Koulibiac

This classic dish is traditionally made with home-made puff pastry and fresh salmon. I have simplified the recipe by using those very easy frozen ready-rolled puff pastry sheets so you won't need to get your rolling pin out. Although fresh salmon has become more affordable now, nothing can beat the simplicity of tinned salmon which can be mixed with long-grain rice, onion, parsley and lemon to make an attractive and tasty dish for a more special occasion.

SERVES 4

50 g (2 oz) long-grain rice
25 g (1 oz) butter or margarine
1 medium onion, peeled and finely chopped
1 × 400 g (14 oz) tin chopped tomatoes, drained
1 × 200 g (7 oz) tin salmon, flaked

1 tablespoon chopped fresh parsley
Juice of ½ lemon
½ teaspoon salt
Freshly ground black pepper
2 ready-rolled sheets puff pastry
1 egg, beaten

Pre-heat the oven to gas mark 6, 200°C (400°F).

Cook the rice in boiling salted water for about 10 minutes, then drain. Melt the butter or margarine in a small pan and sauté the onion until softened. Add the tomatoes and cook gently for 5 minutes. Leave to cool. Add the salmon, rice, parsley and lemon juice and season with salt and pepper. Place one of the pastry sheets on a lightly wetted baking tray. Pile the cooled fish mixture on to the pastry, to within 5 mm (½ in) of the edge. Brush the edges with beaten egg and place the second sheet of pastry over the filling. Seal the edges well and mark with a fork. Make 2 or 3 slits in the pastry to allow any steam to escape. Brush evenly with beaten egg and bake the koulibiac in the oven for about 20 to 25 minutes until the pastry is golden brown and well risen. Serve with a green salad and minted new potatoes.

To freeze: cool, cover and freeze for up to 3 months.

To defrost: overnight in the fridge then re-heat in the oven at gas mark 5, 190°C (375°F) for 15–20 minutes.

Haddock and Onion Quiche

⊹

That useful ready-made flan case is put to the test again for this tasty quiche – I always avoid pastry making when time is short. Concentrate instead on the preparation of the filling of lightly poached smoked haddock or cod in a yoghurt-based custard. The yoghurt has a slightly thicker texture so will take a little less time to cook than a conventional milk-based custard.

SERVES 4

1 × 200 g (7 oz) ready-made flan case
225 g (8 oz) smoked haddock fillets, skinned
150 ml (5 fl oz) milk
Salt and freshly ground black pepper

1 bunch spring onions, finely chopped
2 eggs, beaten
150 ml (5 fl oz) natural yoghurt
A few drops of tabasco sauce

Pre-heat the oven to gas mark 5, 190°C (375°F) and lightly grease a baking sheet.

Place the flan case on the baking sheet. Place the smoked haddock and milk in a small saucepan and season with salt and pepper. Poach the fish gently until a white milky fluid is seen between the flakes. When cooked, drain the fish, reserving the milk. Flake the haddock and combine with the spring onions.

Beat the eggs in a basin and add the reserved poaching milk and the yoghurt. Sprinkle in a few drops of tabasco sauce to taste and season with salt and pepper. Mix in the fish and onions then pour the mixture into the flan case. Bake in the oven for 25 to 30 minutes until set and golden brown. Serve with a mixed salad and coleslaw.

This recipe is not suitable for freezing.

Fish Cake Bake

❖

I hope you enjoy this handy version of fish cakes. Instead of shaping the cakes individually, it saves time to make one large fish cake from the scone mixture. You can use any white fish, but I have made mine with tuna, adding some finely chopped spring onions for extra bite.

SERVES 4

1 × 200 g (7 oz) tin tuna, drained	50 g (2 oz) fresh breadcrumbs
400 g (14 oz) cooked mashed potato	Salt and freshly ground black pepper
3 spring onions, finely chopped	1 egg, beaten
1 tablespoon chopped fresh parsley	2–3 tablespoons vegetable oil

Place the tuna in a large mixing bowl. Add the potatoes, spring onions and parsley. Stir in the breadcrumbs and season with salt and pepper. Add enough egg to bind the mixture together. Heat the oil in a medium-sized frying pan and spread the fish mixture evenly over the base of the pan. Cook over a medium heat for 5 to 10 minutes until the base is well browned and crisp. Cut the fish cake in to 4 pieces, flip each slice over using a spatula and cook the other side. Serve the fish cake from the pan with peas and carrots or courgettes.

This recipe is not suitable for freezing.

Curried Kedgeree

❖

Kedgeree is a tasty breakfast or brunch dish, usually made with a curry sauce as a base, into which are stirred the rice, flaked fish and hard-boiled eggs. I find tuna an excellent substitute for the smoked fish, and with a sprinkling of curry powder into some single cream you can create your own quick curry sauce.

SERVES 4

225 g (8 oz) long-grain rice

2 × 200 g (7 oz) tins tuna,
  drained and flaked

2 hard-boiled eggs, chopped

½ teaspoon curry powder

3 tablespoons single cream

3 tablespoons chopped fresh
  parsley

Salt and freshly ground
  black pepper

Cook the rice in boiling salted water for about 10 minutes until tender. Drain. Stir the tuna and hard-boiled eggs into the rice, sprinkle with curry powder then stir in the cream and parsley. Season with salt and pepper. Cover the pan and heat the kedgeree gently until piping hot. Serve immediately.

This recipe is not suitable for freezing.

Poultry Dishes

Chicken and turkey are now widely available in our butchers' shops, but it is in the supermarket that the wide choice of poultry becomes clear to us. There are drumsticks, breast portions, thighs, legs, not to mention the baby poussins and free-range birds. Although poultry today is very tender, it does rather lack flavour so it makes sense to buy corn-fed or free-range birds which have a superior flavour. If you are stuck with a rather bland bird, however, there are lots of suggestions for dressings, marinades, stuffings and accompaniments in this chapter – all with the added bonus that they include lots of ways to save time and effort. All of the recipes are for chicken or turkey, but you can substitute any suitable game birds in season.

Most of us still enjoy a traditional Sunday lunch, but with smaller families it may not be practicable to buy a whole bird, so do try my version using chicken portions. You will find a tasty lasagne, using pre-cooked sheets of lasagne and an 'all-in-one' sauce. I have also simplified the classic recipe for Chicken Chasseur (page 64) by simmering the flavouring ingredients together first – this cuts out the lengthy reduction of the stock which is part of the classic method. I have also used a similar method for the French classic recipe Coq au Vin (page 67). You can even cut out the preliminary sealing of the meat if you pop the chicken straight into the casserole – this will reduce the calorie content of the dish considerably too. With my quick but tasty Curried Turkey Drumsticks (page 67) and ideas for a simple Mediterranean meal, I hope you'll find there are plenty of short-cut chicken and turkey ideas for you and your family.

Spicy Chicken Drumsticks

If you haven't time to marinate your chicken don't worry – this version shows that it is possible actually to cook the chicken in the marinade ingredients. By removing the chicken skin and making several slits through the flesh you will allow the flavours to penetrate right through and the meat will take on a delicious flavour. This recipe has always been a particular favourite at family barbecues, with the only criticism being that there is never enough.

SERVES 4

8 chicken or turkey drumsticks, skinned
1½ tablespoons apricot jam
1 tablespoon Worcestershire sauce
3 tablespoons tomato ketchup

1 tablespoon soy sauce
1 teaspoon Dijon mustard
1 large clove garlic, peeled and crushed
Salt and freshly ground black pepper

Pre-heat the oven to gas mark 5, 190°C (375°F).

Make several slits through the flesh of the drumsticks and place them in a small roasting tin or ovenproof baking dish. Mix together the apricot jam, Worcestershire sauce, tomato ketchup, soy sauce, mustard and garlic.

Spoon the sauce over the chicken, making sure the pieces are well covered. Cover with a piece of foil or a lid. Bake in the oven for about 25 minutes. Remove the foil or lid, baste the chicken with the sauce and cook uncovered for a further 10 minutes. The sauce will begin to caramelize. The spicy chicken is excellent as part of a barbecue, or served with a crisp green salad.

This recipe is not suitable for freezing.

Stuffed Chicken

❖

Everyone loves Sunday lunch but it is often not practical or economical to buy a whole chicken. This is my short-cut Sunday lunch, using chicken portions which are stuffed with a tasty combination of spinach, Ricotta cheese and garlic. It is a moist filling which permeates the flesh during cooking. For special occasions I like to use the leg with the thigh portions attached – sometimes called Marylands. Thighs or drumsticks work just as well, too. Serve with roast potatoes, julienne carrots and courgettes.

SERVES 4

4 chicken portions
100 g (4 oz) frozen spinach, thawed
2 cloves garlic, peeled and crushed
100 g (4 oz) Ricotta cheese or cottage cheese
Grated rind of ½ lemon
Salt and freshly ground black pepper
25 g (1 oz) butter or margarine, melted

Pre-heat the oven to gas mark 4, 180°C (350°F).

Sieve the spinach, or squeeze it to remove any excess liquid. Mix the spinach with the garlic, Ricotta or cottage cheese and grated lemon rind. Season well with salt and pepper.

You will now need to loosen the skin on the chicken. Slide your fingers under the chicken skin as far as you can without tearing it. Divide the filling into 4, and push the stuffing into the little pocket you have made. Arrange the chicken portions in an ovenproof dish. Brush generously with melted butter or margarine and bake in the oven for 40 to 45 minutes until cooked through and golden brown.

This recipe is not suitable for freezing.

Citrus Chicken

❖

I have devised this recipe to show that you don't need to marinate meat and poultry for hours to achieve a depth of flavour. I have adapted the marinade technique by using a combination of orange juice and Worcestershire sauce. This is spooned over chicken pieces which are then cooked in a tightly-sealed foil parcel. The finished chicken tastes just as though it has been marinated overnight because all the juices remain in the foil parcel. The extra bonus is, of course, you won't have any washing up.

SERVES 4

25 g (1 oz) butter or margarine
1 small onion, peeled and finely chopped
4 tablespoons Worcestershire sauce

2 teaspoons tomato purée
Grated rind and juice of 1 large orange
Salt and freshly ground black pepper
4 chicken portions

Pre-heat the oven to gas mark 6, 200°C (400°F).

Melt the butter or margarine in a small pan and sauté the onion until softened but not brown. Add the Worcestershire sauce, tomato purée, orange rind and juice, stir well and season with salt and pepper. Bring the sauce to the boil, then remove from the heat. Take 4 pieces of foil, double thickness if it is rather thin. Place a chicken joint on each piece of foil and spoon the sauce over the chicken. Seal up the foil parcels tightly, making sure that the sauce cannot escape. Place the foil parcels in a shallow baking dish with the joins facing uppermost. Bake in the oven for about 30 minutes, then open the foil parcels carefully – they will be very hot. Baste the chicken pieces with the sauce, then continue cooking uncovered for a further 15 to 20 minutes. Pierce the chicken pieces at the end of the cooking time. The juices should run clear. The chicken is good served with jacket potatoes and seasonal vegetables.

This recipe is not suitable for freezing.

Crunchy Chicken
with 'Thirty-Second' Marinade

❖

A marinade usually requires several ingredients to achieve that unique flavour. For this marinade, all you need is a bottle of Worcestershire sauce. It does help if you can leave the chicken overnight in the sauce, but if I am in more of a rush than usual, the recipe works well if you simply cook the chicken in the marinade. You can use thighs, drumsticks, or chicken breasts for a special occasion.

SERVES 4

4 chicken portions	50 g (2 oz) sesame seeds
150 ml (5 fl oz) Worcestershire sauce	1–2 tablespoons vegetable oil

Make several slits, using a sharp knife, across the surface of the chicken. Ensure that you cut right into the flesh to allow the marinade to penetrate. Select a suitable dish, one which allows you to pack the chicken portions tightly together and deep enough to hold the marinade. Spoon the Worcestershire sauce over the chicken and baste 2 or 3 times. Cover with cling-film or foil and refrigerate overnight or leave for several hours, basting the chicken from time to time. Preheat the oven to gas mark 5, 190°C (375°F).

Drain off the marinade and press the sesame seeds into the chicken. Place chicken portions in an ovenproof dish or a shallow roasting tin, basting with a little vegetable oil. Bake in the oven for about 25 to 30 minutes until the chicken is thoroughly cooked through.

This recipe is not suitable for freezing.

Turkey and Ham Lasagne

If you use the pre-cooked sheets of lasagne and prepare an all-in-one sauce you will find this dish much less fiddly than the traditional recipe with the more involved béchamel sauce. It is also an excellent way of using up that left-over turkey.

SERVES 6

3 tablespoons vegetable oil
1 large onion, peeled and chopped
2 cloves garlic, peeled and crushed
2 × 400 g (14 oz) tins chopped tomatoes with herbs
1½ teaspoons dried basil
Salt and freshly ground black pepper
75 g (3 oz) plain flour
900 ml (1½ pints) milk

75 g (3 oz) butter or margarine
100 g (4 oz) Cheddar cheese, grated
225 g (8 oz) cooked turkey, chopped
175 g (6 oz) cooked ham, diced
10 sheets easy-cook spinach lasagne
175 g (6 oz) Mozzarella cheese, sliced

Pre-heat the oven to gas mark 4, 180°C (350°F).

Heat the oil and fry the onion and garlic for about 5 minutes over a medium heat. Add the tomatoes, breaking up any larger pieces, and simmer for about 15 minutes. Add the basil and season with salt and pepper.

Meanwhile make the sauce. Place the flour in a saucepan, whisk in the milk and add the butter or margarine in flakes. Season with salt and pepper. Bring the sauce to the boil over a medium heat, whisking continuously until the mixture thickens. Cook for about 1 minute. Stir in the cheese, turkey and ham. Place a layer of turkey sauce at the bottom of a shallow rectangular ovenproof dish. Top with a layer of pasta, then spread some of the tomato and garlic sauce on top. Continue layering the turkey sauce, pasta and tomato sauce ending with a layer of the tomato sauce. Arrange the slices of Mozzarella cheese on top of the lasagne. Bake in the oven for 40 to 45 minutes. This recipe is not suitable for freezing.

Chicken Chasseur

Many of the classic French dishes, including this one, rely for their success on a home-made stock followed by a lengthy reduction of the sauce, to achieve that unique flavour. Most of us want the flavour without the fuss, so I have devised this unusual short-cut method. The chopped tomatoes, tomato purée, apple juice and cider vinegar, onion, garlic and seasoning are simmered together first. This gives you an intensely-flavoured marinade to which you can add the chicken, which makes up for not using the classic method. The apple juice adds a unique taste to the dish and the cider vinegar sharpens up the sauce and also helps to tenderize the chicken. The dish will freeze well – do make sure that it is piping hot and bubbling when re-heated.

SERVES 4

1 × 400 g (14 oz) tin chopped tomatoes
3 tablespoons tomato purée
150 ml (5 fl oz) apple juice
2 tablespoons cider vinegar
1 bouquet garni
1 onion, peeled and finely chopped
2 cloves garlic, peeled and crushed
Salt and freshly ground black pepper
4 chicken legs
100 g (4 oz) button mushrooms
Chopped fresh parsley to garnish

Pre-heat the oven to gas mark 6, 200°C (400°F).

Place the tomatoes, tomato purée, apple juice, cider vinegar, bouquet garni, onion and garlic in a large pan and season with salt and pepper. Stir well, then bring to the boil and simmer for 5 minutes. Remove the pan from the heat and pour the stock mixture into an ovenproof dish. Add the chicken pieces and mushrooms. Cover tightly with a lid or foil. Cook in the oven for about 1 to 1¼ hours until the chicken is thoroughly cooked through. The juices will run clear when the chicken is pierced at its thickest part. Serve with courgettes sautéed in tomato purée, baby carrots and wholegrain rice or new potatoes tossed in butter and fresh basil. Garnish with the parsley.

To freeze: cool quickly, cover and freeze for up to 3 months.
To defrost: overnight at cool room temperature then re-heat thoroughly.

Chicken Casserole with Garlic Sausage

---- ✥ ----

I have included this recipe to show that you don't necessarily need long slow cooking to achieve a mellow-flavoured casserole. My chicken casserole uses finely diced chicken, and an all-in-one sauce flavoured with diced garlic sausage. The result is very tasty, and I hope you will agree with me that it is possible to produce an excellent dish in half the time it takes to cook a 'proper' casserole.

SERVES 4

1 tablespoon vegetable oil
450 g (1 lb) chicken, finely diced
40 g (1½ oz) butter or margarine
100 g (4 oz) mushrooms, sliced

25 g (1 oz) plain flour
300 ml (10 fl oz) milk
50 g (2 oz) garlic sausage, diced
Salt and freshly ground black pepper

Heat the oil in a medium saucepan and gently sauté the chicken for about 10 minutes until evenly browned. You will need to stir the chicken from time to time to prevent it from sticking. Remove the chicken when cooked. Drain, and wipe out the pan with kitchen paper. Add the butter or margarine to the pan and sauté the mushrooms for about 3 minutes.

Next make the sauce. Sprinkle the flour over the mushrooms, whisk in the milk and bring the mixture to the boil, whisking constantly until thickened. Stir in the garlic sausage then return the chicken to the pan and season with salt and pepper. Turn down the heat, cover and simmer gently for about 5 minutes. Serve with fettuccine noodles and courgettes.

To freeze: cool quickly, cover and freeze for up to 3 months.
To defrost: overnight in the fridge then re-heat thoroughly.

Mediterranean Chicken

In this recipe the chicken, sauce and vegetables are all cooked together in a foil parcel – eliminating the need for washing up several saucepans. The cream cheese melts during cooking creating an unusual but simple sauce not only for the chicken but also for the vegetables.

SERVES 4

1 tablespoon olive oil
4 chicken breast portions
75 g (3 oz) low fat cheese
225 g (8 oz) courgettes,
   thinly sliced
1 × 200 g (7 oz) tin chopped
   tomatoes, drained
Salt and freshly ground
   black pepper
½ tablespoon dried oregano

Pre-heat the oven to gas mark 6, 200°C (400°F).

Cut 4 pieces of foil about 25 cm (10 in) square and brush lightly with oil. With a sharp knife, make 2 or 3 cuts across each chicken breast. Push a little cream cheese into the slits. Arrange the chicken on the foil. Divide the courgettes and tomatoes between the foil parcels. Sprinkle with salt, pepper and oregano. Wrap the parcels up tightly, sealing well, to ensure that all the juices remain intact. Place the parcels in a roasting tin or baking dish. Cook in the oven for about 30 to 40 minutes until the chicken is cooked through.

This recipe is not suitable for freezing.

Curried Turkey Drumsticks

— ✥ —

This is a real short-cut cheats curry. Simply mix crushed potato crisps with curry powder and use to coat turkey breasts or drumsticks. It's a very effective way of achieving that unique flavour normally obtained by longer slower cooking.

SERVES 4

100 g (4 oz) plain potato crisps	4 tablespoons semi-skimmed milk
2–3 teaspoons curry powder	8 turkey drumsticks, skinned

Pre-heat the oven to gas mark 6, 200°C (400°F) and lightly grease a baking sheet.

Place the crisps in a mixing bowl and crush with the end of a rolling pin. They need to be in fairly rough pieces, not too powdery and fine. Stir in the curry powder and mix well. Place the milk in a small basin and dip in the drumsticks, ensuring they are evenly covered. Roll the drumsticks in the crispy curry mixture until well coated. Place the turkey on the baking sheet. Cook in the oven for about 25 to 30 minutes until golden brown. Serve with a green salad.

This recipe is not suitable for freezing.

Coq au Vin

— ✥ —

This classic dish usually requires several lengthy stages of preparation. First of all you need a home-made stock, then the shallots or onions need to be caramelized, and the resulting sauce needs to be reduced to achieve the unique flavour. I have by-passed these processes and still managed to achieve a dish with an excellent flavour. The short-cut technique I use is to simmer the red wine with the onion, garlic, herbs and stock initially, and I have found that this creates the base for a robustly flavoured Coq au Vin. It is also unnecessary to seal the chicken joints in hot oil before adding to the casserole. Finally if you find yourself really short of time, why not use pickled onions as I have done – they help to cut out all that fiddly peeling. Don't worry when you come to eat the casserole, the pungent taste of the pickled onions has disappeared. Bon appétit!

SERVES 4

1 × 225 g (8 oz) jar pickled onions, drained
1 bouquet garni
2 cloves garlic, peeled and crushed
1 teaspoon concentrated vegetable stock
600 ml (1 pint) red wine
4 chicken breasts, thighs or drumsticks

4 rashers smoked back bacon, de-rinded and diced
150 g (5 oz) button mushrooms
Salt and freshly ground black pepper
1 tablespoon cornflour

Pre-heat the oven to gas mark 4, 180°C (350°F).

Place the onions, bouquet garni, garlic, stock and wine in a large pan. Bring the mixture slowly to the boil. Reduce the heat and simmer for 5 minutes only. Pour the sauce into an ovenproof dish. Add the chicken portions, chopped bacon and mushrooms and season with salt and pepper. Cover the casserole and cook in the oven for about 1 to 1¼ hours. If the sauce needs to be thickened, mix the cornflour with a little water and stir it into the casserole about 10 minutes before the end of the cooking time. Stir well to ensure the sauce is smooth. Serve with gratin dauphinoise (page 29).

To freeze: cool quickly, cover and freeze for up to 3 months.
To defrost: overnight at cool room temperature then re-heat thoroughly.

Chicken and Ham Jambalaya

It is always handy to have some short-cut recipes for using left-overs. A jambalaya is usually made using uncooked meats, poultry and fish. I have adapted this traditional New Orleans dish, with its colourful jumble of ingredients, to make use of left-over chicken or ham. All you need is one large pan big enough to hold all the ingredients and you can produce a tasty supper dish within half an hour. It is important to make sure that the chicken is thoroughly cooked and not just warmed through.

SERVES 4

2 tablespoons vegetable oil
1 large onion, peeled and chopped
1 red pepper, de-seeded and chopped
1–2 cloves garlic, peeled and crushed
150 ml (5 fl oz) dry white wine
450 ml (15 fl oz) chicken stock

1 × 400 g (14 oz) tin tomatoes, drained
1 teaspoon dried thyme
1 teaspoon dried basil
A few drops of tabasco sauce
350 g (12 oz) American long-grain rice
450 g (1 lb) cooked chicken, cubed
175 g (6 oz) cooked ham, cubed

Heat the oil in a large pan or flameproof casserole. Add the onion, pepper and garlic and fry over a medium heat until softened. Don't allow the onion to brown. Add the wine, 300 ml (10 fl oz) of the stock, the tomatoes, herbs and tabasco sauce. Carefully stir in the rice, chicken and ham and bring the mixture slowly to the boil. Cover the pan with a lid, reduce the heat and simmer for 20 to 25 minutes until the rice is tender. You may find you need to add more stock. The finished dish should have absorbed most of the liquid. The rice is cooked when the grains are easily crushed between your thumb and forefinger. Serve with hunks of French bread or pitta bread.

This recipe is not suitable for freezing.

Iced Chicken in Quick Lemon Sauce

————— ✥ —————

The first time I served this dish was to a group of friends after an open-air play at Ludlow Castle in Shropshire. It was one of those rare balmy evenings and the chilled chicken went down a treat. Traditionally the lemon sauce for this delicious summer-time dish is made using the stock in which the chicken has been poached. In this short-cut version, a tangy lemon sauce – which tastes just as good – is created by combining Greek yoghurt, soured cream and mayonnaise. These ingredients have just the right creamy consistency and are very easy to mix together. I have used a lemon flavouring, but you could add curry powder or chilli, depending on your taste.

SERVES 6

1.5 kg (3½ lb) chicken
1 onion, peeled

6 peppercorns
2 bay leaves

FOR THE SAUCE

150 ml (5 fl oz) soured cream
150 ml (5 fl oz) Greek yoghurt
150 ml (5 fl oz) mayonnaise
Salt and freshly ground black pepper

Finely grated rind of 2 lemons
Juice of 1 lemon
½ cucumber, peeled and diced
225 g (8 oz) seedless grapes
2 sticks celery, finely chopped

FOR THE GARNISH

1 red apple, sliced
1 green apple, sliced

1 tablespoon lemon juice

Place the chicken in a large saucepan. Pour in enough cold water just to cover the chicken and add the onion, peppercorns and bay leaves. Bring to the boil. Turn down the heat, cover and simmer for about 1 hour or until the chicken juices run clear when pierced at the thickest point. Remove the chicken from the pan. Cool it quickly, strip the flesh from the carcass, and cut into bite-sized pieces. Cool the stock and freeze for soup-making at a later date.

Place the soured cream, yoghurt and mayonnaise in a medium-sized basin and season with salt and pepper. Add the lemon rind and juice and mix well to combine the flavours together. Stir the chicken pieces, cucumber, grapes and celery into the lemon sauce. Cover and refrigerate well. The chicken should be served well chilled. Garnish with alternate slices of red and green eating apples tossed in a little lemon juice. Serve with warm crusty rolls and salad.

This recipe is not suitable for freezing.

Meat Dishes

Although at first sight it would appear to be impossible to cook many meat dishes quickly – apart from simple grilled or fried meats – I have devised several short-cuts which will reduce the preparation and cooking time of several well known traditional recipes without losing any of the essential flavour associated with them.

Apart from the more obvious and expensive cuts, cooking meat is by its nature a more lengthy process, but flavoursome meat meals are the cornerstone of family meals, and we do need to be able to by-pass some of the lengthier processes where possible.

In this respect basic recipes are always useful in any repertoire, so I have devised a Tasty Meat Sauce (page 73) which is so versatile it is possible to create not one but five other dishes from it. Using the short-cut store cupboard, the tasty meat sauce can become a moussaka, a lasagne, a cottage pie, a cobbler or a chilli con carne as well as being used as a sauce for pasta.

If you do find yourself with some cooking time in the kitchen, it's a good idea to prepare a bulk batch of the meat sauce – some to use immediately and the rest to be frozen to form the basis of the other five dishes. So by using tinned kidney beans, which don't need to be soaked overnight, and ready-cooked sheets of lasagne you can quickly rustle up a chilli or a lasagne. In addition, the lengthy process of mashing potatoes for a cottage pie can be shortened by making use of grated potato as a topping for the meat sauce. If a cobbler is your choice, then instead of making a scone topping it is just as easy to use chunks of French bread.

A hearty casserole is always a good family standby, so I hope you will enjoy the two short-cut classic recipes in this section: Beef and Orange Carbonnade (page 87) and Goulash (page 80) – made with sun-dried tomatoes. I have adapted these recipes by by-passing the usual method of sealing the meat first and reducing the stock, in favour of simmering the flavouring ingredients together first, which will give you the base for a richly tasting sauce. I'm sure you will find the results successful.

Ethnic foods are always popular, so I have included the classic Indian recipe, Biriani (page 84), which is normally made by layering up partly cooked rice and partly cooked meat mixture, which is then cooked for a fairly long time in the oven. My short-cut version uses minced lamb instead of the more usual cubed lamb, which speeds up the cooking time considerably. In addition, I fully cook the rice and meat sauce, and continue the cooking process for only a short time in the oven. I'm sure you will agree, the result is very tasty, and so much healthier than buying a chilled ready-prepared version.

A steak and kidney pie is always a family favourite but if you make use of those easy-to-handle frozen puff pastry sheets, this dish is something which can be on the table much more quickly than if you had to make your own pastry.

Tasty Meat Sauce

This is my ultimate short-cut meat recipe because I use it as a base to create moussaka, lasagne, cottage pie, cobbler or chilli con carne. It even doubles up as a Bolognese sauce to serve with pasta. I have reduced the meat content slightly and introduced some red lentils, which do not need soaking as many pulses do. The lentils will also act as a thickening agent so you won't need to mix flour or cornflour – another time-saver.

Always buy the best quality mince you can afford as cheaper mince can be very fatty. If it appears to have too many white flecks then disregard it in favour of a pack with an even red colour. To save time, make double quantities and freeze one portion for a later meal.

SERVES 6

2 tablespoons vegetable oil
1 large onion, peeled and finely chopped
1 clove garlic, peeled and crushed (optional)
100 g (4 oz) streaky bacon, de-rinded and chopped
350 g (12 oz) good quality minced beef
1 × 400 g (14 oz) tin chopped tomatoes with herbs
75 g (3 oz) red lentils

2 medium carrots, peeled and sliced
100 g (4 oz) mushrooms, sliced
2 tablespoons Worcestershire sauce
2 tablespoons tomato purée
½ teaspoon dried mixed herbs
Salt and freshly ground black pepper
300 ml (10 fl oz) beef stock or red wine

Heat the oil in a large pan, add the onion and garlic, if using, and cook until softened but not brown. Stir in the bacon and minced beef. Break the mince up by stirring with a wooden spoon, and cook gently until the meat turns brown. Stir in the tomatoes, lentils, carrots, mushrooms, Worcestershire sauce, tomato purée and herbs and season with salt and pepper. Finally add the stock or wine and stir well to combine all the ingredients. Place a lid on the pan and simmer for 40 to 45 minutes, stirring from time to time until the mixture is cooked and has thickened slightly.

Use the meat sauce to create the following recipes: Moussaka (page 75); Lasagne (page 76); Crunchy Cottage Pie (page 77); Beef Cobbler (page 78); Chilli con Carne (page 79).

To freeze: cool, cover and freeze for up to 4 months.
To defrost: overnight in the fridge then re-heat thoroughly.

Moussaka

You will probably find that many moussaka recipes call for the aubergines to be salted and left for up to 1 hour to extract their moisture and to reduce any bitterness. They are often then sautéed in oil before being added to the dish. In my quick moussaka, the sliced aubergines are simply placed in a large mixing bowl and covered with boiling water. This softens and blanches them and makes any other preparation unnecessary. I do love aubergines. Not only do they look beautiful with their taut shiny skins, but they taste delicious too. Very fresh aubergines have several sharp prickly protrusions at the stem end, which can give you a nasty stab if you are not careful, but at least you will know they are in peak condition.

SERVES 6

1 quantity Tasty Meat Sauce (page 73)
3 medium aubergines, sliced
225 g (8 oz) cream cheese or low fat cream cheese

4 tablespoons milk
2 eggs, beaten
50 g (2 oz) Cheddar cheese, grated (optional)

Pre-heat the oven to gas mark 4, 180°C (350°F).

Make up the meat sauce following the recipe on page 73.

Place the aubergines in a large bowl and cover with boiling water. Drain. Mix the cream cheese with the milk and eggs until you have a smooth sauce. Arrange a layer of aubergine slices on the bottom of an ovenproof dish. Cover with a layer of meat sauce, then continue layering until all the meat and aubergines have been used, finishing with a layer of aubergine. Pour a layer of cheese sauce over the moussaka, and sprinkle with cheese, if using. Bake in the oven for 40 to 45 minutes until the moussaka is bubbling and golden brown. Serve with a crisp green salad and Soda Bread (page 107).

This recipe is not suitable for freezing.

Lasagne

❖

A lasagne is a favourite supper-time dish in our family, but because it requires making in several stages it can be time-consuming. I cut the corners in two ways, firstly I always buy the ready-cooked sheets of lasagne – but do remember to check the label on the packet first. Then instead of making a traditional cheese sauce I make a sauce using yoghurt mixed with egg, which cuts out all that lengthy stirring. If you can leave the lasagne to stand for 10 minutes before baking it does help all the flavours to develop – but if you are in a hurry this is not essential. I use my food processor for making quick work of mixing the cheese, yoghurt and eggs.

SERVES 6

1 quantity Tasty Meat Sauce (page 73)
225 g (8 oz) cottage cheese
150 ml (5 fl oz) natural yoghurt
2 eggs, beaten
Salt and freshly ground black pepper
8 sheets easy-cook spinach lasagne
75 g (3 oz) Cheddar cheese, grated

Pre-heat the oven to gas mark 4, 180°C (350°F) and grease a large rectangular ovenproof dish.

Make up the meat sauce following the recipe on page 73.

Mix together the cottage cheese, yoghurt and eggs until well combined. Season with salt and pepper.

Pour a layer of meat sauce in the base of the dish. Cover with 2 or 3 sheets of the lasagne – you may need to break them to ensure an even fit.

Add another layer of the meat sauce, followed by the rest of the lasagne sheets. Pour the cheese sauce over the meat and pasta layers, making sure that the pasta is well covered, otherwise it can be a little chewy when cooked. Sprinkle with the cheese. Cook in the oven for 30 to 40 minutes until the lasagne is bubbling and golden brown. Serve with hunks of French bread and a mixed salad.

To freeze: cool, cover and freeze for up to 3 months.
To defrost: overnight in the fridge then re-heat thoroughly.

Crunchy Cottage Pie

⊹

A cottage pie is always a family favourite, but peeling, boiling and mashing potatoes can be time-consuming. Why not try my alternative to creamed potatoes. Simply peel and grate the potatoes – using your food processor for extra convenience – and mix with grated cheese, and you have fast and easy crunchy topping with no messy saucepan to wash up.

SERVES 6

1 quantity Tasty Meat Sauce (page 73)
1 kg (2 lb) potatoes, peeled and grated
100 g (4 oz) Cheddar cheese, grated
2 tablespoons chopped fresh parsley
Salt and freshly ground black pepper
1 tomato, sliced
2 sprigs parsley

Pre-heat the oven to gas mark 4, 180°C (350°F).
Make up the meat sauce following the recipe on page 73.
Place grated potato in a colander and rinse with plenty of cold water. This removes a lot of the starch and will eliminate any powdery taste in the finished topping. Tip the washed potato on to a clean tea towel and dry off as much moisture as you can by squeezing the cloth. Tip the potato into a mixing bowl. Add 75 g (3 oz) of the grated cheese and the parsley and season with salt and pepper. Mix well. Place the meat sauce in an ovenproof dish. Pile the potato topping over the meat mixture and level out with a fork but don't press down too much. Sprinkle with the remaining cheese. Bake in the oven for 35 to 40 minutes until the meat mixture is bubbling and the potato is golden brown. Garnish with tomato and parsley and serve with seasonal vegetables.

To freeze: do not add the topping. Cool, cover and freeze for up to 4 months.

To defrost: overnight in the fridge then re-heat thoroughly before adding the topping as described above.

Beef Cobbler

A cobbler is traditionally made with a scone topping, but when time is short, why not try topping it with hunks of French bread instead. Simply spread generous slices of baguette with garlic butter, then pile with grated cheese and pop under the grill to toast until bubbling. The result is very attractive, and you will have a crisp and crunchy topping in minutes. Serve the dish with buttered and peppered seasonal cabbage – my favourite vegetable.

SERVES 6

1 quantity Tasty Meat Sauce (page 73)

1 small French stick or use half a large stick and use the rest to mop up the juices from the meat sauce

50 g (2 oz) butter or margarine

1–2 cloves garlic, peeled and crushed

100 g (4 oz) Red Leicester cheese, grated

Pre-heat the grill.

Make up the meat sauce following the recipe on page 73.

Slice the French stick. Cream the butter or margarine until softened then beat in the garlic. Spread the garlic butter over the slices of French bread. Pour the piping hot meat sauce into a large casserole dish and arrange the French bread on top of the sauce. Sprinkle the grated cheese over the bread. Place the cobbler under the hot grill for about 5 minutes until the cheese is bubbling and golden brown. Serve immediately.

To freeze: do not add the topping. Cool, cover and freeze for up to 4 months.

To defrost: overnight in the fridge then re-heat thoroughly before adding the topping as described above.

Chilli con Carne

I make no apologies for serving this dish when I entertain friends for lunch or supper and I find that it tastes even better if you make it the day before you need it then re-heat it thoroughly. Tinned kidney beans are so quick and convenient to use as they don't need any soaking overnight. Do remember to drain and rinse them first, though, as the liquid in which they are canned has an unpleasant metallic taste. Red kidney beans are high in fibre and rich in protein, and added to the meat sauce will create a robust dish for a variety of occasions.

SERVES 6

1 quantity Tasty Meat Sauce (page 73)
1–2 teaspoons chilli powder
1 × 300 g (11 oz) tin red kidney beans, drained and rinsed

Follow the recipe for the Tasty Meat Sauce on page 73, but once the onion and garlic have cooked and softened, sprinkle with chilli powder according to taste. Cook gently to release the flavour before adding the bacon and minced beef. Continue with the recipe as detailed. Twenty minutes before the end of the cooking time, stir in the kidney beans, mix thoroughly, and continue cooking until the chilli is piping hot. Serve with nutty wholegrain rice and a crispy green salad.

To freeze: cool, cover and freeze for up to 4 months.
To defrost: overnight in the fridge then re-heat thoroughly.

Sun-Dried Tomato Goulash

❖

Another classic dish, usually calling for a home-made stock and a well reduced sauce to achieve the unique taste. However, I find that my technique of simmering the flavouring ingredients together first, before adding the meat, gives an excellent result. The sun-dried tomatoes are a real treat – they are so tasty and add a wonderful pungency to the dish.

SERVES 4

2 tablespoons tomato purée
1 tablespoon paprika
2 cloves garlic, peeled and crushed
1 teaspoon concentrated vegetable stock
600 ml (1 pint) water
1 onion, peeled and finely chopped
1 red or orange pepper, de-seeded and finely chopped

3–4 sun-dried tomatoes in olive oil, drained and chopped
450 g (1 lb) lean braising steak, finely cubed
Salt and freshly ground black pepper
150 ml (5 fl oz) natural yoghurt or soured cream

Place the tomato purée, paprika, garlic and stock in a saucepan. Gradually blend in the cold water. Bring to the boil and simmer for 5 minutes to allow the flavours to develop. Add the onion, pepper, sun-dried tomatoes and steak and season with salt and pepper. Continue to cook, covered, on top of the stove for about 1 hour, stirring from time to time. Alternatively turn the casserole into a large ovenproof dish, cover and cook for about 1½ hour at gas mark 4, 180°C (350°F).

When the braising steak is tender, stir in the yoghurt or soured cream.

Serve with pasta and seasonal vegetables.

To freeze: do not add the yoghurt or soured cream. Cool, cover and freeze for up to 4 months.

To defrost: overnight in the fridge then re-heat thoroughly before adding the yoghurt or soured cream as described above.

Sausage and Bean Stew
❖

I find canned beans extremely useful because they do not need lengthy overnight soaking. If you keep a selection of canned beans in your short-cut store cupboard, you can quickly create a nourishing family supper. This dish is also a good way of stretching a small amount of meat.

SERVES 6

2–3 tablespoons olive oil
1 onion, peeled and finely chopped
1 green chilli pepper, de-seeded and finely chopped
1 red pepper, de-seeded and diced
1 orange pepper, de-seeded and diced
1 × 300 g (11 oz) tin red kidney beans, drained and rinsed

1 × 425 g (15 oz) tin borlotti beans, drained and rinsed
1 × 425 g (15 oz) tin chick peas, drained and rinsed
350 g (12 oz) garlic sausage, peeled and sliced
2 × 400 g (14 oz) tins chopped tomatoes
2 tablespoons Worcestershire sauce
Salt and freshly ground black pepper

Heat the oil and fry the onion and chilli pepper gently for about 5 minutes until softened but not brown. Add the peppers and cook for a further 3 to 4 minutes, stirring occasionally. Add the drained beans and peas, garlic sausage, tomatoes and Worcestershire sauce and season with salt and pepper. Bring gently to the boil, reduce the heat, cover and simmer for 25 to 30 minutes, stirring occasionally.

This recipe is not suitable for freezing.

Steak and Kidney Pie

— ✥ —

This pie represents the epitome of good British home cooking. It is a hearty and warming dish, but can be time-consuming, with both the pastry and the meat to prepare and cook. If I am in a hurry I have to admit it's an effort to make my own pastry, so I always use bought puff pastry because it's so good. However, it's worth shopping around to find the particular brand you like best. I find the ready-rolled puff pastry sheets ideal topping for pies and you will find them in the freezer section of your local supermarket. They are good because there is no waste, and because they are baked separately and served with the meat, they will not become soggy from the gravy. Don't be put off by the ingredients list for the meat sauce – once it's in the pan it will virtually look after itself.

SERVES 4

25 g (1 oz) butter or margarine

1 tablespoon vegetable oil

450 g (1 lb) lean braising steak, finely cubed

100 g (4 oz) kidneys, finely cubed

1–2 garlic cloves, peeled and crushed

100 g (4 oz) button mushrooms

150 ml (5 fl oz) beef stock

150 ml (5 fl oz) brown ale

1 bay leaf

½ teaspoon dried thyme

1 tablespoon tomato purée

1½ tablespoons plain flour

3 tablespoons cold water

200 g (7 oz) ready-rolled puff pastry sheets or puff pastry

1 egg, beaten

1 tablespoon sesame seeds

Pre-heat the oven to gas mark 6, 200°C (400°F) and lightly grease a baking sheet.

Melt the butter or margarine with the oil and sauté the braising steak and kidney until evenly browned. Stir in the garlic and mushrooms and cook for 5 minutes, stirring from time to time. Gradually add the beef stock, brown ale, bay leaf and thyme, and finally the tomato purée. Cover the pan and simmer for about 1½ hours or until the meat is tender. Blend the flour and water together then stir it into the pan to thicken the sauce.

Meanwhile take 2 or 3 sheets of the ready-rolled pastry. Cut across diagonally to make 4 triangles. Lift the pastry triangles on to the baking sheet. Brush with a little beaten egg and sprinkle with sesame seeds. Bake in the oven for 15 to 20 minutes until the pastry is well risen and golden brown. Spoon the meat mixture on to individual serving plates with a triangle of puff pastry alongside.

To freeze: cool, cover and freeze the pie filling for up to 4 months. To defrost: overnight in the fridge then re-heat thoroughly before adding the pastry as described above.

Pork with Prunes

This is a variation on the classic French dish Porc aux Pruneaux. My version uses no-need-to-soak prunes, which saves on the lengthy overnight soaking with the usual dried prunes. Fruit is always particularly succulent when used in casseroles, and the prunes absorb the flavour of the apple juice which I have used instead of the usual stock. The use of apple juice also helps to marinate the meat and speed up the tenderizing process.

I find it unnecessary to seal the meat first in hot oil, the recipe works just as well if you place the meat straight into the casserole dish. You will also reduce the calorie content of the dish, too.

The dish freezes well, and will actually improve in flavour. Make sure that the casserole is re-heated thoroughly. It should be piping hot and bubbling in the centre.

SERVES 4

450 g (1 lb) casserole pork, cubed

2 tablespoons vegetable oil

1 clove garlic, peeled and crushed

1 large onion, peeled and sliced

250 ml (8 fl oz) apple juice

100 g (4 oz) no-need-to-soak prunes

2 tablespoons brandy (optional)

½ level teaspoon dried thyme

Salt and freshly ground black pepper

Pre-heat the oven to gas mark 4, 180°C (350°F).

Place the pork in an ovenproof casserole. Place the oil in a frying pan, add the garlic and onion and cook gently until softened but not brown. Spoon into the casserole dish. Drain off the remaining oil and wipe out the pan with kitchen paper. Add the apple juice, prunes, brandy, if using, and thyme to the pan and season with salt and pepper. Bring to the boil, then pour over the onion and pork in the dish. Place a piece of foil over the casserole dish followed by a lid to seal the casserole tightly and ensure the flavours are retained. Cook in the oven for about 1½ hours until the pork is tender. If you need to thicken the sauce, blend 2 to 3 teaspoons of cornflour with a little apple juice and stir well into the casserole about 15 minutes before the end of cooking. Serve with nutty wholegrain brown rice or new potatoes, broccoli or purple sprouting.

To freeze: cool, cover and freeze for up to 4 months.
To defrost: overnight in the fridge then re-heat thoroughly.

Biriani

Traditionally served on special occasions, biriani is a very popular Indian dish. It is usually made by layering up partly cooked basmati rice and curry sauce, which are then cooked in the oven in a casserole dish.

In this short-cut version, the cooking time is reduced considerably by using minced lamb instead of the usual cubed lamb. To make up for the shorter cooking time which could affect the development of the flavours, the garlic, ginger, spices and onion are processed together first before adding to the meat to give a concentrated flavour. I have also eliminated one of the stages in the preparation of the biriani. I fully cook, rather than partly cook, the rice and the curry sauce, and you will find you can reduce the cooking time of the dish in the oven.

SERVES 4

2 tablespoons vegetable oil
2 garlic cloves, peeled
1.5 cm (½ inch) cube fresh root ginger, grated
1 onion, peeled and quartered
2 teaspoons ground cumin
2 teaspoons ground coriander
6 cardamoms, crushed
½ teaspoon chilli powder

450 g (1 lb) lean minced lamb
1 × 400 g (14 oz) tin tomatoes, drained
750 ml (1¼ pints) vegetable stock
225 g (8 oz) basmati rice
150 ml (5 fl oz) natural yoghurt
1 tablespoon sultanas
1 tablespoon flaked almonds

Place the oil, garlic, ginger, onion, cumin, coriander, cardamoms and chilli powder in a food processor or blender and process until you have a smooth paste. Place the spiced paste into a large pan. Add the minced lamb and cook, stirring frequently, until the meat is browned. Stir in the tomatoes and 150 ml (5 fl oz) of stock. Bring to the boil, cover and simmer for 30 to 35 minutes until the lamb is cooked through, stirring from time to time to prevent sticking.

Meanwhile cook the rice in the remaining stock for about 25 minutes. The grains should be soft when squashed between your thumb and forefinger. When the curry sauce and rice are ready, layer up in a casserole dish, drizzling the rice layers with yoghurt. Cook the biriani in the oven for about 20 minutes until heated through. Garnish with sultanas and nuts and serve with a tomato and onion side salad.

This recipe is not suitable for freezing.

Sausage Cassoulet

❖

The classic haricot bean stew originating from France is a fine dish, but with several lengthy cooking and preparation processes is certainly not to be attempted if you want to eat in a hurry as it can take up to 3 hours to cook. This version reduces that time by one-third. It uses tinned cannellini beans instead of dried haricot beans which require overnight soaking. The original recipe also uses belly pork which takes a long time to cook as it is a fairly tough cut of meat. I have used lean bacon instead and a selection of quick-cooking low fat sausages which will impart their own particular flavour to the dish. In addition, by using garlic cloves, canned tomatoes with herbs and bay leaves, you can still achieve the flavours normally associated with the lengthy cooking of the classic cassoulet.

SERVES 4

2 tablespoons vegetable oil

2 medium onions, peeled and sliced

2 cloves garlic, peeled and crushed

2 sticks celery, sliced

2 medium carrots, peeled and thinly sliced

225 g (8 oz) low fat beef sausages

225 g (8 oz) low fat pork sausages

225 g (8 oz) lean smoked bacon, de-rinded and chopped

2 bay leaves

2 tablespoons tomato purée

450 ml (15 fl oz) beef stock

1 × 400 g (14 oz) tin chopped tomatoes with herbs

1 × 425 g (15 oz) tin cannellini beans, drained and rinsed

75 g (3 oz) fresh wholemeal breadcrumbs

1 tablespoon chopped fresh parsley

Pre-heat the oven to gas mark 4, 180°C (350°F).

Heat the oil in a large pan or flameproof casserole. Add the onions, garlic, celery and carrots. Cook over a medium heat until the vegetables are softened but do not allow them to brown. If necessary, transfer the vegetables to an ovenproof casserole dish. Cut the sausages into 3 or 4 pieces. Place the sausages, bacon, bay leaves and tomato purée in the casserole dish with the vegetables. Gradually stir in the stock followed by the tomatoes, beans, breadcrumbs and parsley. Stir all the ingredients gently to mix. Cover with a lid and cook in the oven for about 1 hour. You will find that the sausages swell as they absorb the stock. Serve with spring greens and carrots.

This recipe is not suitable for freezing.

Beef and Orange Carbonnade

—————— ⟴ ——————

This is my adaptation of an old Flemish recipe. Normally when making a casserole, the meat and accompanying vegetables are sealed first in hot oil before being transferred to the casserole. I find this unnecessary and prefer to simmer the flavouring with the stock or Guinness which creates a kind of intense marinade, resulting in a robustly flavoured casserole – the Guinness also helps to tenderize the meat. This is also a much healthier method, cutting out the unnecessary use of oil. Try to buy the best quality beef you can afford – it will cut down the cooking time.

SERVES 4

600 ml (1 pint) Guinness
2 onions, peeled and
  chopped
2 cloves garlic, peeled and
  crushed
2–3 carrots, sliced
1 bouquet garni
Grated rind and juice of
  1 orange
300 ml (10 fl oz) vegetable
  stock
Salt and freshly ground
  black pepper

450 g (1 lb) lean braising
  steak, finely cubed
2 rashers smoked back
  bacon, de-rinded and
  finely chopped
2 tablespoons cornflour
4 tablespoons cold water
4 slices crusty bread
25 g (1 oz) butter or
  margarine
1 tablespoon French
  mustard

Pre-heat the oven to gas mark 4, 180°C (350°F).

Place the Guinness, onions, garlic, carrots, bouquet garni, orange rind and juice and stock in a large saucepan and season with salt and pepper. Bring to the boil then reduce the heat, cover and simmer gently for 5 minutes. Stir the meat and bacon into the sauce then transfer it to a large ovenproof casserole, cover and cook in the oven for about 2 hours. This will depend on the tenderness of the beef. Mix together the cornflour and water and stir in to thicken the sauce.

Meanwhile cut the slices of bread into 2. Mix together the butter or margarine with the mustard and spread on the bread. When the beef is tender, place the slices of bread on top of the casserole, mustard side up, and place under a pre-heated grill for 5 minutes or until bread is toasted. Serve the casserole piping hot with braised red cabbage.

To freeze: do not add the topping. Cool, cover and freeze for up to 4 months.
To defrost: overnight in the fridge then re-heat thoroughly before adding the topping as described above.

Desserts

For many families, cheese and biscuits, yoghurt, fruit and ice-cream provide enough variety to finish everyday meals. However, for a more special occasion a well chosen dessert or pudding can be the highlight of a meal, providing an opportunity for the host or hostess to serve something stunning. All this takes time, though, so in this chapter you will find a selection of short-cuts for some of the classic favourites and the more traditional puddings.

Gelatine is widely used in cheesecakes, but can be temperamental and fiddly, so why not try my gelatine-free version. It will not keep for as long, but if made and eaten the same day will be excellent. If you want to serve a fruit salad, then the preparation of the fruit can be cut to a minimum by using a dried fruit salad mixture. Soak the fruit in fruit juice, wine or liqueur, chill it well, and it will provide a succulent finish to any meal.

I think even Granny would approve of the short-cut versions of her old favourites, Eve's Pudding (page 96) – which makes use of a one-stage cake mixture instead of the creaming method – and the Bread and Butter Puddings (page 92) which are baked in individual ramekin dishes to speed up the cooking process. Also if the milk is heated up first instead of being used cold you will find it soaks into the bread much quicker. It is even possible to serve a short-cut version of that favourite nursery pudding, Rice Pudding (page 94), by cooking the mixture on the hob instead of the lengthier slow baking.

If you and your family enjoy home-made ice-cream you can even short-cut the traditional method of making ice-cream, which normally uses a syrup or a custard base, by simply whipping up cream and yoghurt. The choice of flavours will depend on the family's preference, but select from a combination of nuts, chocolate, dried fruit, fresh fruit or anything else you fancy and you probably won't buy ice-cream again.

Don't feel guilty about using ready-made pastry cases – they are perfect for the Yorkshire Curd Tart (page 97), and the Tarte au Citron (page 98).

Tarte Tatin

This is the classic upside-down apple tart usually made with a rich buttery pastry which requires careful handling, and a caramel sauce, which as everyone knows can be fiddly and temperamental. In this short-cut version, the fruit and sugar are caramelized together first in a saucepan and I have used the new frozen rich shortcrust pastry which is just as good as home-made.

SERVES 4

25 g (1 oz) butter or margarine
50 g (2 oz) fine demerara
  sugar
2 eating apples, peeled,
  cored and thinly sliced

2 dessert pears, peeled,
  cored and thinly sliced
225 g (8 oz) frozen rich
  shortcrust pastry

Pre-heat the oven to gas mark 6, 200°C (400°F) and line an 18 cm (7 in) cake tin.

Melt the butter or margarine and sugar together in a saucepan. Pour the mixture into the base of the cake tin. Arrange the apple and pear slices on top of the butter and sugar mixture. Roll out the pastry to a circle just larger than the size of the cake tin and place the pastry on top of the arranged fruit. Bake in the oven for 20 minutes until the pastry is golden brown. Turn out, fruit side up, on to a serving plate and serve hot with cream, natural yoghurt or fromage frais.

This recipe is not suitable for freezing.

Nut and Chocolate Chip Ice-Cream

There are lots of low fat creams on the market which are ideal for my short-cut ice-cream recipes, which mean you can still enjoy a treat for half the calories. If you find you enjoy a sweeter version, just add a little extra honey.

SERVES 4

150 ml (5 fl oz) low fat whipping cream	2 tablespoons runny honey
250 ml (8 fl oz) natural yoghurt	50 g (2 oz) chocolate chips
	50 g (2 oz) chopped mixed nuts

Whip together the cream and yoghurt until the mixture holds its shape. Stir in the honey, followed by the chocolate chips, then the nuts. Pour the mixture into a freezer container and freeze until firm. Leave in the fridge for 1 hour to soften before serving.

This recipe can be kept in the freezer for up to 4 months.

Butterscotch Sauce

This is always a favourite spooned over home-made ice-cream – and very speedily made from store cupboard ingredients.

SERVES 4

50 g (2 oz) butter or
  margarine

4 tablespoons soft brown sugar
2 tablespoons golden syrup

Place all the ingredients in a heavy-based saucepan. Heat very gently until all the sugar has dissolved. Bring the mixture to the boil for about 3 to 5 minutes or until the mixture begins to thicken. Pour into a heatproof basin to cool. Drizzle over home-made ice-cream.

This recipe is not suitable for freezing.

Mini Bread and Butter Puddings

One of Granny's favourites and it's so delicious you'll want to tuck into it quickly. A worthwhile time-saving technique is to heat the milk first to speed up the cooking time, and I also find you can reduce the usual rather lengthy cooking time by baking the puddings in individual ramekin dishes.

SERVES 4

3–4 thin slices bread or fruit
  bread, buttered
50 g (2 oz) currants or
  sultanas
1 tablespoon caster sugar

Grated rind of 1 orange
450 ml (15 fl oz) milk
2 eggs, beaten
A pinch of freshly grated
  nutmeg

Pre-heat the oven to gas mark 5, 190°C (375°F).
  Cut the bread into strips. Arrange, buttered side up, in individual ramekins, sprinkling with currants or sultanas between the layers.

Place the sugar, orange rind and milk in a saucepan. Heat gently, but do not boil. Whisk the warm milk into the beaten egg. Pour into a jug and strain over the bread and fruit. Sprinkle with nutmeg. Bake the puddings in a roasting tin half-filled with warm water for 20 minutes or until the custard has set.

This recipe is not suitable for freezing.

Citrus and Ginger Cheesecake
✥

Traditionally cheesecakes have been made with gelatine which many of my students and friends say they have problems with, but this recipe will give you the light texture of the cheesecake filling without using gelatine. I do agree that coping with gelatine can be fiddly and time-consuming, so I hope you will enjoy this gelatine-free, low fat version of this popular dessert.

SERVES 4

200 g (7 oz) gingernuts

90 g (3½ oz) butter or margarine, melted

225 g (8 oz) low fat cream cheese

225 g (8 oz) cottage cheese, sieved

Grated rind of 1 lemon

Grated rind and juice of 1 orange

50 g (2 oz) caster sugar

Crush the ginger biscuits and mix with the melted butter or margarine.

Using the back of a spoon, press the mixture into the base of a 20 cm (8 in) flan ring. Place in the freezer for 20 minutes, or chill whilst making the filling. Mix together the cream cheese, cottage cheese, lemon rind, orange rind and juice and the caster sugar. Spoon the filling into the biscuit base and smooth the top. Refrigerate until ready to serve. Use within a few hours of making.

This recipe is not suitable for freezing.

Apricot and Banana Brûlée

✥

Traditional Crème Brûlée is made with a rich combination of egg yolks and cream, requiring lengthy cooking and stirring in a double boiler. This light and healthy version is one my mum uses regularly and it's so quick. Any combination of fruit can be used – fresh seasonal fruit is especially good. Use scissors to snip up the apricots.

SERVES 4

2 large ripe bananas, sliced and tossed in a little lemon juice

2 tablespoons no-need-to-soak apricots, finely chopped

2 tablespoons orange juice

250 ml (8 fl oz) fromage frais

4 tablespoons demerara sugar

Pre-heat the grill.

Divide the fruit between 4 ramekin dishes. Drizzle the orange juice over the fruit. Stir the fromage frais, and spoon over the fruit. Sprinkle with the demerara sugar. Grill until the sugar caramelizes. Cool and chill until required.

This recipe is not suitable for freezing.

Creamy Raspberry Rice Pudding

✥

My husband has always been a big rice pudding fan. Probably spurred on by memories of visits to his uncle's farm in the Yorkshire Dales when his old favourite, made with milk from the herd of Friesians and enriched with fresh farm eggs, was frequently on the menu. This up-dated version short-cuts the traditional lengthy baking and is cooked on the hob for speed. It has raspberry flavoured fromage frais stirred through it.

SERVES 4

40 g (1½ oz) pudding rice	150 ml (5 fl oz) raspberry
600 ml (1 pint) milk	fromage frais
1 tablespoon runny honey	
A pinch of freshly grated	
nutmeg	

Place the rice, milk, honey and nutmeg in a saucepan. Bring gently to the boil and then lower the heat and simmer very gently for 25 to 30 minutes or until the rice is tender and most of the liquid has been absorbed.

Stir the rice from time to time to prevent it sticking. If necessary top up the pan with a little extra milk. Remove the pan from the heat and stir in the fromage frais. Heat through gently but do not allow it to boil. Serve at once.

This recipe is not suitable for freezing.

Cinnamon Fruit Salad

A fruit salad is always a refreshing finish to a meal, but the peeling and slicing of the fruit can be time-consuming if you are in a hurry. This version uses a dried fruit salad mix, easily found in health food shops or in the supermarket, and which needs very little preparation. As an extra treat, add some slices of fresh banana.

SERVES 4

250 g (9 oz) dried fruit salad	Grated rind of 1 lemon
mix	2 medium bananas
200 ml (7 fl oz) apple juice	Fromage frais or low fat
2 sticks cinnamon	natural yoghurt

Chop the larger pieces of dried fruit if necessary and place in a saucepan. Add the apple juice, cinnamon and lemon rind. Bring to the boil, then simmer gently for 10 to 15 minutes until the fruit is softened. Pour the fruit and juice into a pyrex bowl. Cool then refrigerate.

The fruit salad is best served well chilled. Just before serving slice the bananas into the fruit salad. Serve with fromage frais or Greek yoghurt.

This recipe is not suitable for freezing.

Eve's Pudding

❖

Traditional granny's favourite puddings have undergone a revival lately. This classic warming pudding is made with a one-stage sponge, piled on to fluffy Bramley apples.

SERVES 4

450 g (1 lb) Bramley apples, peeled, cored and finely sliced
150 g (5 oz) soft brown sugar
Grated rind and juice of 1 lemon

1 tablespoon water
75 g (3 oz) soft margarine
1 egg
100 g (4 oz) self-raising flour
A little milk to mix (optional)

Pre-heat the oven to gas mark 5, 190°C (375°F) and grease an ovenproof dish.

Slice the apples finely into the dish. Sprinkle with 50 g (2 oz) of the brown sugar, lemon rind and juice and water. Place the margarine, the remaining sugar, the egg and flour in a mixing bowl and beat using an electric mixer or place all the ingredients in a food processor and process for about 15 seconds. Add a little milk to the mixture, if necessary, to give a soft dropping consistency. Spoon the creamed mixture over the apples. Bake in the oven for 40 to 45 minutes until the apples are tender and the sponge mixture is well risen and golden brown.

To freeze: cool, cover and freeze for up to 4 months.
To defrost: overnight in the fridge then re-heat at gas mark 4, 180°C (350°F). Cover with foil if the sponge begins to brown too much.

Lemon Sauce Pudding

I have fond memories of my mum's light sponge puddings smothered with creamy custard. This is the ultimate short-cut recipe. Using one lot of ingredients, you magically end up with a sponge pudding with its own built in sauce, as the pudding separates out into two layers.

SERVES 4

Grated rind and juice of 1 lemon	100 g (4 oz) caster sugar
50 g (2 oz) butter or margarine	2 eggs, separated
	50 g (2 oz) self-raising flour
	300 ml (10 fl oz) milk

Pre-heat the oven to gas mark 5, 190°C (375°F) and grease a large ovenproof dish.

Place the lemon rind, butter or margarine and sugar in a mixing bowl and beat until light and fluffy. Gradually beat in the egg yolks, followed by the flour.

Stir in the milk and lemon juice. Whisk the egg whites until stiff and standing in peaks. Fold carefully into the creamed mixture and pour into the greased dish. Stand the dish in a roasting tin filled with 1 cm (½ in) of hot water. Bake in the oven for about 45 minutes until the pudding is set and spongy to the touch, and the lemon sauce has separated out. Serve hot.

This recipe is not suitable for freezing.

Yorkshire Curd Tart

If you visit Yorkshire you will find this unusual tart on sale in bakers' shops from the Pennine hills to the east coast. My husband loves to eat it straight from the oven – but beware, you will need to follow behind with the vacuum! This is my shortened version – a one-stage pastry as opposed to the rubbing in method, which results in a pleasing crumbly texture. Also if you stand your tart tin on a metal baking sheet the pastry will cook through quicker and you won't need to bake it blind.

SERVES 4

100 g (4 oz) soft margarine
1 tablespoon chilled water
175 g (6 oz) plain flour
150 g (5 oz) Yorkshire curds
  or cottage cheese
40 g (1½ oz) caster sugar
2 eggs, beaten

2 tablespoons single cream
50 g (2 oz) currants
2 drops of almond essence
Grated rind of ½ lemon
A pinch of freshly grated
  nutmeg

Pre-heat the oven to gas mark 6, 200°C (400°F) and grease an 18 cm (7 in) flan ring.

Cream together margarine, water and 2 tablespoons of flour in a mixing bowl. Mix in the remaining flour and knead the mixture lightly until smooth. Roll out the pastry into a large enough circle to line the flan tin.

Combine all the remaining ingredients except the nutmeg. Mix well. Pour into the prepared flan tin, then sprinkle with nutmeg. Place the flan tin on to a metal baking sheet and bake in the oven for 20 minutes or until the tart is evenly browned and set.

This recipe is not suitable for freezing.

Tarte au Citron
———————— ✥ ————————

As a dedicated Francophile I couldn't resist including another classic. The traditional Tarte au Citron uses a very rich buttery pastry, which can be tricky to handle and needs frequent chilling between stages. The filling is baked in the pastry case and requires a long slow cooking time. My version uses a ready-made pastry case, and I find you achieve a very good result by making a home-made lemon curd in a saucepan. To help your lemons yield more juice, roll them on the worktop with the palm of your hands a few times.

SERVES 6

225 g (8 oz) caster sugar
3 eggs or 6 egg yolks
Grated rind and juice of
    2 lemons

75 g (3 oz) butter or
    margarine, cubed
1 × 18 cm (7 in) ready-made
    pastry case

Place all the ingredients in a saucepan and mix well together. Gradually bring to simmering point, stirring continuously. Allow to thicken.

Pour through a sieve into a bowl, cover and cool. Pour the cooled curd into the flan case and smooth the surface.

Serve with Greek yoghurt, crème fraîche or fromage frais.

This recipe is not suitable for freezing.

Lemon Meringue Pie

Use the lemon curd from the previous recipe to make a lemon meringue pie by whisking up a couple of egg whites and sugar and piling on to the lemon filling.

1 quantity lemon curd
    (page 98)
1 ready-made 18 cm (7 in)
    pastry case

2 egg whites
75 g (3 oz) caster sugar

Pre-heat the oven to gas mark 5, 190°C (375°F).

Pour the lemon curd into the pastry case. Whisk egg whites in a clean, grease-free bowl until stiff. Whisk in half the sugar then fold in the remainder. Pile the meringue on to the lemon curd. Bake in the oven for about 10 minutes until the meringue is evenly brown. Serve hot or cold.

This recipe is not suitable for freezing.

Meringue and Ginger Ice-Cream

❖

Ice-creams are traditionally made either by making an egg custard as a base for the cream and flavouring or by preparing a sugar syrup – but neither of these methods are very practicable if you want fast, easy ice-cream. You can achieve the same texture and flavour using cream, half cream, yoghurt or fromage frais as a base. I'm always being asked for these recipes. The possibilities for varying the flavours are endless and you won't need to stir them.

SERVES 6

300 ml (10 fl oz) low fat whipping cream
300 ml (10 fl oz) Greek yoghurt or fromage frais
6 pieces stem ginger, chopped
3 tablespoons ginger syrup
6 meringues, broken up

Whip together the cream and yoghurt until floppy and the mixture hangs off the whisk. Stir in the stem ginger, ginger syrup and broken meringues. Place the mixture into a pudding basin, loaf tin or polythene box lined with lightly oiled cling-film. Freeze. Leave the ice-cream in the fridge for 1 hour to soften before serving.

This recipe can be kept in the freezer for up to 4 months.

Baking

The art of home baking is undergoing a bit of a revival lately, having been out of fashion for several years. In the meantime, though, there has been a growth in the volume of ready-made cakes and biscuits available, which unfortunately, although convenient, do tend to be heavily over-processed, synthetic and generally lacking in any real flavour. If home baking has taken a back seat in your household lately, you could join the revival of the art by trying out some of these home baking short-cuts.

From a health point of view it is not advisable that cakes and biscuits should form too regular a part of our diet, but there can't be many of us who don't relish the thought of a slice of home-made cake, or nibbling on a crisp biscuit from time to time.

In a busy day, it can be difficult to find time for a baking session, so this section relies heavily on the ever popular all-in-one method of cake-making. The availability of soft margarines means that you can whip up a cake in minutes, and so by-pass the lengthier creaming process. The possibilities for varying the flavours and textures are endless and you will find a selection of loaves and cakes full of ready-to-eat fruit, apricots and dates, nuts and also fresh fruit, too. If you keep your short-cut store cupboard stocked with a selection of baking ingredients, it becomes very easy to provide cakes and biscuits for a variety of occasions such as packed lunches, picnics or tea-time. I tend to use wholemeal flour where I can as it has a nutty texture and flavour. I also prefer to use soft brown sugar for the same reason.

The food processor is my biggest short-cut asset, though. Once you have weighed out the ingredients, you can quickly process a cake mixture in seconds. If you hate the thought of lining cake tins, do look out for the ready-cut circles of greaseproof and silicone paper and thin rolls of paper for the edges – these will save you time and trouble. They are widely available in good kitchen shops and supermarkets.

Cakes and biscuits freeze extremely well, so I always do a batch bake and pop a few loaves or cakes in the freezer, so I always have something to hand in an emergency.

There is nothing nicer than a kitchen filled with the aroma of baking, and bread-making, so I do hope you will enjoy spoiling your family with some of these short-cut cakes and biscuits.

Victoria Sandwich

This is a classic all time favourite tea-time treat which never fails to please, but I prefer this all-in-one version as opposed to using the usual creaming method. My version uses less sugar – preferably the soft brown variety – and healthy nutty wholewheat flour.

Bake the cake in a loaf tin and top with low fat cream cheese mixed with a little icing sugar and you'll have a real up to the minute old favourite.

It's a good idea to make double quantities of the mixture as it does freeze very well.

MAKES 1 × 20 cm (8 in) CAKE

100 g (4 oz) soft margarine	½ teaspoon baking powder
100 g (4 oz) soft dark brown sugar	2 eggs
100 g (4 oz) wholewheat self-raising flour	

FOR THE TOPPING

100 g (4 oz) low fat cream
  cheese
1 tablespoon icing sugar

2 tablespoons apricot jam
6 walnut halves

Pre-heat the oven to gas mark 4, 180°C (350°F) and line and grease a loaf tin.

Place all the cake ingredients in a mixing bowl and beat for 1 to 2 minutes until you have a soft dropping consistency. Spoon into the tin and level the surface.

Bake in the oven for 25 to 30 minutes until well risen and golden brown. Leave to cool.

When cool, split the cake horizontally and sandwich together with apricot jam. Mix together the cream cheese and icing sugar and spread over the top of the cake. Decorate with a few walnuts.

To freeze: before filling and decorating, cool, wrap and freeze for up to 3 months.
To defrost: approximately 4 hours at cool room temperature.

VARIATIONS

Coffee and Walnut Cake
Try adding 50 g (2 oz) finely chopped walnuts, plus 1 tablespoon instant coffee powder mixed with 2 teaspoons of hot water to the mixture.

All-in-One Chocolate Sponge
Add 1 tablespoon of cocoa powder to the mixture.

All-in-One Lemon or Orange Sponge
The fresh tang of citrus is wonderful in this easy cake. Add the grated rind of 1 lemon or 1 orange plus a tablespoon of the juice to the mixture.

The rest of the juice can be used to mix with the icing sugar for the topping or you can drizzle it into the cake whilst it is still warm.

Make double the quantity and split and vary the flavourings.

Ginger and Apricot Loaf

—————— ✥ ——————

No-need-to-soak fruit is the ultimate short-cut, so that there is no need for overnight marinating to obtain the flavour. This moist and fruity loaf uses ready-to-eat apricots spiced up with ginger – though you could use dates instead and vary the flavour by adding the zest of a lemon to the mixture. Snip up the apricots with scissors for speed. The loaf is made in minutes and will disappear even faster!

MAKES 1 × 450 g (1 lb) LOAF

100 g (4 oz) self-raising flour	2 eggs, beaten
2 teaspoons ground ginger	100 g (4 oz) no-need-to-soak
100 g (4 oz) soft brown sugar	apricots, roughly chopped
100 g (4 oz) soft margarine	50 g (2 oz) sultanas

Pre-heat the oven to gas mark 4, 180°C (350°F) and grease and base line a 450 g (1 lb) loaf tin.

Mix the flour and ginger in a bowl then add the sugar, margarine and eggs. Beat for 1 to 2 minutes until you have a soft dropping consistency. Carefully fold in the fruit. Spoon the mixture into the tin, level the surface and bake for about 35 to 40 minutes until golden brown. The cake will shrink away from the sides slightly and a skewer inserted into the centre will come out clean.

To freeze: cool, wrap and freeze for up to 3 months.
To defrost: overnight at cool room temperature.

Flapjack

—————— ✥ ——————

I have included Flapjack as the classic quick and easy biscuit. It is a real one-pan wonder, but if you want to make it even faster, then try using bought muesli base. The sweet moist oaty biscuit also makes an unusual simple topping for fruit puddings instead of the usual crumble.

MAKES 12

175 g (6 oz) butter or margarine

100 g (4 oz) soft light brown sugar

4 tablespoons golden syrup

300 g (11 oz) rolled oats

75 g (3 oz) raisins

Pre-heat the oven to gas mark 4, 180°C (350°F) and lightly grease and base line a 20 cm (8 in) square cake tin.

Place the butter or margarine, sugar and syrup in a saucepan and heat gently for 2 to 3 minutes until the butter or margarine has melted and the sugar has dissolved. Remove the pan from the heat. Stir in the oats and raisins and mix well. Spoon mixture into the tin and bake in the oven for about 20 minutes until golden brown. Cut into bars whilst still warm. Leave the flapjack to cool in tin before removing.

VARIATIONS

Fruit Flapjack
Instead of the raisins, use a mixture of no-need-to-soak dates and coconut, and stir into the mixture with the oats.

Ginger and Chocolate Flapjack
Use the syrup from a jar of stem ginger instead of the golden syrup, and 4 pieces of stem ginger, roughly chopped. In addition, add 2 tablespoons of cocoa with the oats and mix together well. When the flapjack is cool, spread with 100 g (4 oz) melted chocolate for an extra special touch.

Nutty Flapjack
Fold 50 g (2 oz) of chopped mixed nuts and 50 g (2 oz) unsalted peanuts into the oat mixture.

This recipe is not suitable for freezing.

Crunchy Apricot Bars

❖

If you don't want to eat bought preservative-full biscuits, but have no time to make your own, do try these delicious no-bake biscuits. Once the ingredients have been mixed, they simply need to be chilled in the fridge. If you've ever wanted to find a use for all those left-over cereals in the cupboard, these nibbles should fit the bill.

MAKES 18

100 g (4 oz) butter or margarine	75 g (3 oz) branflakes
50 g (2 oz) soft brown sugar	75 g (3 oz) cornflakes
4 tablespoons honey	50 g (2 oz) no-need-to-soak apricots

Lightly grease and base line a 30 × 20 × 2.5 cm (12 × 8 × 1 in) Swiss roll tin.

Melt the butter or margarine, sugar and honey in a pan over a low heat for about 2 minutes until the sugar has completely dissolved. Remove from the heat and stir in the cereals and fruit. Mix thoroughly. Spoon the mixture into the tin and press down gently. Chill for 2 to 3 hours in the fridge. Cut into bars with a sharp knife.

This recipe is not suitable for freezing.

Mixed Fruit Tea Brack

❖

This is another delicious tea bread recipe, with no need for creaming or rubbing in. You don't even have to bother with a mixing bowl – just combine everything together in a large saucepan. It's also a great way of using up left-over tea in the pot – whether it's Earl Grey or China. Eat with a hunk of Wensleydale cheese or any other crumbly white cheese.

SERVES 4

225 g (8 oz) sultanas	150 ml (5 fl oz) hot tea
100 g (4 oz) currants	1 egg, beaten
100 g (4 oz) raisins	225 g (8 oz) self-raising flour
100 g (4 oz) soft brown sugar	

Pre-heat the oven to gas mark 3, 160°C (325°F) and grease and line a 900 g (2 lb) loaf tin.

Place the dried fruit, sugar and hot tea in a large saucepan, stir well and simmer gently for about 5 minutes. Remove from the heat and leave to cool. Mix in the beaten egg and fold in the flour. Stir until well combined.

Spoon the mixture into the prepared tin and bake in the oven for about 1½ to 1¾ hours until the cake is well risen and golden brown. Test with a skewer or a knitting needle to see if it is fully cooked through in the centre. If the loaf looks as though it is browning too much place a piece of foil on top. Cool and store in an airtight tin.

To freeze: cool, wrap and freeze for up to 3 months.
To defrost: overnight at cool room temperature.

Soda Bread

Home-made bread is a tasty accompaniment to lots of meals – whether it's a flavoursome lunch-time soup, or a crisp and crunchy salad – or even better, used to mop up those hard-to-resist juices from a hearty winter casserole. I recently served this bread at a 'girls' lunch and I was amazed at how quickly it disappeared even though everyone insisted they were on a diet! Delicious as it is, it can be very time-consuming even when using the new easy-blend yeast. My family love this quick soda bread. Using bicarbonate of soda and cream of tartar, the mixture rises quickly to produce a light dough.

SERVES 8

450 g (1 lb) plain flour	25 g (1 oz) white vegetable
2 teaspoons bicarbonate of	fat or margarine
soda	2 teaspoons caster sugar
4 teaspoons cream of tartar	300 ml (10 fl oz) milk
1 teaspoon salt	

Pre-heat the oven to gas mark 6, 200°C (400°F) and grease a baking sheet.

Sieve the flour with the cream of tartar and bicarbonate of soda. Mix in the salt. Rub in the fat and stir in the caster sugar. Add the milk and mix to a soft but not sticky dough, kneading lightly. Shape into a round. Place the bread on to the baking sheet and mark into 4 with a sharp knife, but do not cut right through. Bake in the oven for about 30 minutes until well risen and golden brown.

This recipe is not suitable for freezing.

All-in-One
Chocolate Chip Cookies
⚜

Home-made biscuits are a real treat, but rolling and shaping the dough can be fiddly. So why not fill up the biscuit tin with these crunchy cookies which only need brief mixing and dropping on to a baking sheet?

MAKES 20

75 g (3 oz) soft margarine	150 g (5 oz) self-raising flour
75 g (3 oz) soft brown sugar	50 g (2 oz) desiccated
A few drops of vanilla	coconut
essence	50 g (2 oz) chocolate chips
1 egg	

Pre-heat the oven to gas mark 4, 180°C (350°F) and grease, or cover a baking sheet with non-stick paper.

Place all the ingredients into a mixing bowl and mix well until well blended. Spoon the mixture on to the prepared baking sheet and bake in oven for about 12 to 15 minutes. Cool on the baking sheet for about 1 minute before placing on a wire cooling tray to finish cooling.

This recipe is not suitable for freezing.

Orchard Scones

✤

Scones have always been quick to make, so I have not included the recipe itself as a short-cut, so much as the technique for shaping them afterwards. This is a real short-cut in itself and by-passes all that fiddly cutting, rolling and shaping. As a change, try using half white and half wholemeal flour.

SERVES 8

225 g (8 oz) self-raising flour
50 g (2 oz) soft margarine
25 g (1 oz) granulated sugar
2 tablespoons desiccated
  coconut

1 dessert apple, peeled and
  diced
150 ml (5 fl oz) natural
  yoghurt

Pre-heat the oven to gas mark 6, 200°C (400°F) and lightly grease a baking sheet.

Place the flour and margarine in a mixing bowl and rub the fat into the flour. Stir in the sugar and coconut followed by the diced apple. Stir in the yoghurt and mix to a soft but not sticky dough. If the mixture is a little dry add 1 or 2 tablespoons of cold milk. Turn the dough on to a floured board and pat into a round about 2 cm (¾ in) thick.

Lift on to the sheet and mark into 8 sections, but do not cut right through. Bake in the oven for 15 to 20 minutes. Cool on a wire rack. The scones need to be eaten on the same day.

To freeze: cool, wrap and freeze for up to 3 months.
To defrost: overnight at cool room temperature.

Chocolate Brownies

❖

This classic combination of chocolate and nuts always goes down well. I hope you enjoy these short-cut brownies as much as my family do. I have devised this all-in-one tray bake version which is quicker and easier than making individual buns.

MAKES 24

225 g (8 oz) soft margarine
175 g (6 oz) soft brown sugar
4 eggs, beaten
225 g (8 oz) self-raising flour

75 g (3 oz) walnuts, brazil or mixed nuts chopped
100 g (4 oz) good quality milk chocolate, roughly chopped

Pre-heat the oven to gas mark 4, 180°C (350°F) and grease and line a 28 × 23 × 5 cm (11 × 9 × 2 in) Swiss roll tin.

Place all the ingredients except the chocolate in a large mixing bowl. Beat until well mixed then fold in the chopped chocolate. Spread the mixture into the tin, smooth the top and level out. Bake in the oven for 40 to 45 minutes until well risen and golden brown. Cool slightly. Turn out on to a cooling rack and cut into 24 squares.

This recipe is not suitable for freezing.

Cinnamon and Apple Loaf

❖

The addition of apple to this loaf together with a hint of cinnamon will give you a moist and spicy, easy-to-make, easy-to-slice tea-time treat. The recipe will make two loaves – so pop one in the freezer.

MAKES 2 × 450 g (1 lb) LOAVES

225 g (8 oz) wholemeal self-raising flour

100 g (4 oz) soft margarine

50 g (2 oz) soft brown sugar, dark or light variety

2 eggs, beaten

2 tablespoons milk

1 rounded teaspoon ground cinnamon

1 cooking apple, peeled, cored and chopped

FOR THE TOPPING

1 teaspoon ground cinnamon

1 teaspoon demerara sugar

Pre-heat the oven to gas mark 4, 180°C (350°F) and grease and base line 2 × 450 g (1 lb) loaf tins.

Place all the ingredients in a large mixing bowl. Mix thoroughly until well combined and you have a soft dropping consistency. Divide the mixture between the tins and level out. Bake in the oven for about 1 hour until well risen and golden brown. It's a good idea to leave the loaves in the tins for 5 minutes before removing and placing on a cooling rack.

To freeze: cool, wrap and freeze for up to 3 months.
To defrost: overnight at cool room temperature.

Banana and Nut Loaf

Many tea-time loaves are made using the rubbing in method. I have adapted the recipe to produce this easy all-in-one loaf. Bananas keep the loaf moist, but do choose them carefully – they need to be soft enough to mash, but not too brown – save the brown speckled ones for eating! If the fruit is too ripe, the loaf may remain soggy in the middle. Using wholemeal flour and nuts gives the cake an interesting flavour and texture. If you're feeling extravagant, spread a little butter on each slice when cooled.

MAKES 1 × 900 g (2 lb) LOAF

100 g (4 oz) soft margarine	1 teaspoon baking powder
100 g (4 oz) soft light brown sugar	3 medium bananas, mashed
	Grated rind of 1 orange
2 eggs	50 g (2 oz) walnuts, roughly
225 g (8 oz) wholemeal self-raising flour	chopped
	A little warm water

Pre-heat the oven to gas mark 4, 180°C (350°F) and grease and base line a 900 g (2 lb) loaf tin.

Place all the ingredients in a large mixing bowl and beat with an electric mixer for about 1 minute. Alternatively mix everything in a food processor. The mixture should be a soft dropping consistency – if it is a little stiff add a little warm water. Spoon the mixture into the tin; it should half-fill the tin. Bake in the oven for 50 to 60 minutes until a skewer inserted into the centre comes out clean.

This recipe is not suitable for freezing.

No-Bake Chocolate Squares

Of course, the ultimate short-cut cake is one that you don't have to bake at all. This is a real time-saving no-bake cake, and anything chocolatey is always a favourite for special occasions and children's parties.

MAKES 24

120 g (4½ oz) butter or margarine	1 egg, beaten
120 g (4½ oz) soft brown sugar	250 g (9 oz) ginger biscuits, crushed
2 tablespoons cocoa powder	25 g (1 oz) crystallized ginger, coarsely chopped

Melt the butter or margarine and stir in the sugar until dissolved. Add the cocoa powder and stir well. Stir in the beaten egg, followed by the ginger biscuits and the crystallized ginger. Mix together well. Press into a shallow Swiss roll tin and smooth the top. Refrigerate until firm then cut into squares or fingers.

For an extra special finish, try melting 100 g (4 oz) of plain chocolate and spreading over the cake.

This recipe is not suitable for freezing.

Ginger 'n' Spice Fruit cake

❖

Using soft margarine means you can whip up this spicy fruit cake in no time at all, and you will find it just as flavoursome as a cake where the fruit has been soaked for hours in alcohol. You will probably have most of the ingredients in the short-cut store cupboard so you can save time on shopping too.

MAKES 1 × 18 cm (7 in) CAKE

225 g (8 oz) self-raising flour	100 g (4 oz) soft brown sugar
2 teaspoons mixed spice	225 g (8 oz) mixed dried
1 teaspoon ground ginger	fruit
1 teaspoon baking powder	2 eggs, beaten
100 g (4 oz) soft margarine	2 tablespoons milk

Pre-heat the oven to gas mark 3, 160°C (325°F) and grease and line an 18 cm (7 in) round cake tin.

Sieve together the flour, mixed spice, ginger and baking powder in a mixing bowl. Add the rest of the ingredients and beat well for about 1 minute. Alternatively, use the food processor – place all the ingredients except the fruit in the processor and process for 20 seconds, then fold in the fruit by hand. Spoon the mixture into the cake tin and bake in the oven for about 1¼ hours until well risen and golden brown.

To freeze: cool, wrap and freeze for up to 3 months.
To defrost: overnight at cool room temperature.

Cherry and Orange Cake

❖

Using vegetable oil is an invaluable short-cut method to making cakes, with no creaming or rubbing in. The dry ingredients combine easily with the oil to produce a smooth batter. You can use corn oil, sunflower or rape seed oil or any pure vegetable oil but not olive oil or walnut oil; these are strongly flavoured and are best saved for salads.

MAKES 1 × 18 cm (7 in) CAKE

120 ml (4 fl oz) corn oil
2 eggs, beaten
2 tablespoons milk
150 g (5 oz) caster sugar
275 g (10 oz) self-raising
  flour, sieved

A pinch of salt
150 g (5 oz) glacé cherries,
  washed, dried well and
  quartered
Grated rind of 1 orange

Pre-heat the oven to gas mark 4, 180°C (350°F) and grease and line an 18 cm (7 in) cake tin.

In a large bowl, whisk together the corn oil, eggs, milk and sugar until well combined. Fold in the flour, salt, cherries and grated orange rind. Take care that you don't leave any pockets of flour in the mixture.

Pour the batter into the cake tin and bake in the oven for about 1 to 1¼ hours until the centre of the cake springs back when depressed and the top is nicely browned.

To freeze: cool, wrap and freeze for up to 3 months.
To defrost: overnight at cool room temperature.

Honey Cake

❖

This is a wonderful one-stage cake, which means you can by-pass the traditional creaming or rubbing in usually required. The addition of honey gives this cake a very distinctive flavour and a lovely moist texture. It is quickly put together with ingredients to be found in the short-cut store cupboard and great for those times when the cake tin is empty and needs to be refilled quickly. The whisky is optional – a quick tot may help you more than the cake!

MAKES 1 × 20 cm (8 in) CAKE

100 g (4 oz) soft margarine
25 g (1 oz) caster sugar
4 tablespoons runny honey
2 eggs, beaten
175 g (6 oz) wholemeal self-raising flour
A pinch of baking powder
½ teaspoon ground cinnamon
25 g (1 oz) chopped mixed nuts
1 tablespoon whisky or water

Pre-heat the oven to gas mark 5, 190°C (375°F) and grease and line a 20 cm (8 in) cake tin.

Place all the ingredients in a large mixing bowl and beat with an electric mixer for 1 to 2 minutes until it has a soft dropping consistency. Spoon the mixture into the prepared tin and bake in the oven for 25 to 35 minutes until well risen and golden brown and the cake springs back when touched in the centre.

To freeze: cool, wrap and store for up to 3 months.
To defrost: overnight at cool room temperature.

Cheese and Herb Plait

Making bread is something that most of us find difficult to fit in between working, ferrying children, or generally leading very busy lives. There is nothing to beat the wonderful smell of fresh bread, and most of us would agree, bread-making is immensely satisfying. Traditional methods of bread-making rely on the power of the yeast to help the bread to rise. When the yeast, which is a living organism, comes into contact with moisture, warmth and flour, it is stimulated to grow, and produces carbon dioxide gas which makes the dough rise. We are not disputing the fact that bread made with yeast is superb, but you can by-pass all that kneading, pouring and rising of traditional methods, by using this short-cut yeast-free version. It needs to be eaten straight away, but you can vary the taste by adding cheese, herbs, chilli powder, pesto sauce or as a special treat, sun-dried tomatoes.

SERVES 8

25 g (1 oz) butter or margarine	50 g (2 oz) Cheddar cheese, grated
450 g (1 lb) self-raising flour	1 teaspoon dried mixed herbs
2 teaspoons baking powder	1 egg, beaten
1 teaspoon salt	300 ml (10 fl oz) milk

Pre-heat the oven to gas mark 7, 220°C (425°F) and lightly grease a baking sheet.

Rub the fat into the flour and baking powder. Stir in the salt, cheese and herbs. Make a well in the centre of the flour, pour in some of the egg with a little of the milk and gradually work in the dry ingredients. Continue to add the liquid to give a soft manageable dough. Turn dough on to a floured board and roll to a sausage shape.

Make 2 horizontal cuts down the length of the dough and shape into a plait. Place on the baking sheet and bake in the oven for 30 to 35 minutes until well risen and golden brown.

This recipe is not suitable freezing.

Passion Cake

This must be one of the most requested recipes I have ever made, since it made its debut at a cookery demonstration to a group of WI ladies several years ago. It is also a very aptly named cake – once bitten always smitten! No one can quite believe how easy it is to produce such a moist, healthy cake. You can omit the topping if you want a simple cake, or add it to make a delicious dessert.

MAKES 1 × 20 cm (8 in) CAKE

175 ml (6 fl oz) vegetable oil
175 g (6 oz) caster sugar
3 eggs, beaten
1 teaspoon vanilla essence
100 g (4 oz) walnuts, chopped
225 g (8 oz) carrots, coarsely grated

175 g (6 oz) plain flour
1 teaspoon bicarbonate of soda
1 teaspoon baking powder
1 teaspoon ground cinnamon
1 teaspoon salt

FOR THE TOPPING

100 g (4 oz) low fat cream cheese

25 g (1 oz) icing sugar

Pre-heat the oven to gas mark 4, 180°C (350°F) and grease and line a 20 cm (8 in) loose-bottomed cake tin.

Place all the ingredients in a large mixing bowl and beat well until you have a thick and smooth batter. Pour the mixture into the tin and smooth the top. Bake in the oven for about 1¼ hours. Cool on a wire rack.

Beat together the topping ingredients and spread over the cake.

To freeze: cool, wrap and freeze for up to 3 months.
To defrost: overnight at cool room temperature.

Bran Fruit Loaf

❖

Another tasty one-stage loaf, this is perfect for anyone who longs for the taste of home-made food but is very short of time. Breakfast cereal is a great way to begin the day – but this cake proves that you can eat cereal at any time. The bran cereal makes an interesting addition to this loaf and of course it's very healthy too. The fruit and bran need a little soaking, but you could do that whilst clearing the kitchen after breakfast. This loaf will be popular as a mid-morning snack or popped into lunch boxes.

MAKES 1 × 900 g (2 lb) LOAF

100 g (4 oz) All-Bran cereal
150 g (5 oz) soft light brown
  sugar
275 g (10 oz) mixed dried
  fruit

300 ml (10 fl oz) milk
100 g (4 oz) wholemeal self-
  raising flour
½ teaspoon baking powder

Pre-heat the oven to gas mark 4, 180°C (350°F) and grease and line a 900 g (2 lb) loaf tin.

Place the All-Bran, sugar and dried fruit in a large bowl. Pour over the milk, stir well and leave to stand for about 30 minutes so that the bran and fruit absorb the liquid. Add the flour and baking powder and mix well. Spoon into the tin and level the surface. Bake in the oven for 1¼–1½ hours until the loaf is well risen. If you find it is browning too much, cover with a double thickness of greaseproof paper or parchment. Turn out on to a cooling rack.

To freeze: cool, wrap and freeze for up to 3 months.
To defrost: overnight at cool room temperature.

Crunchy Cider Apple Cake

—————— ✤ ——————

This recipe was given to me by a friend. Wholesome favourites, cider, apples, and nuts, provide the base for this delicious cake, which I have adapted from the traditional creaming method. This short-cut method works very well, because the cider makes the mixture easy to handle. Flour does vary in quality, though, so I would advise you not to put all the cider in the mixture to begin with. Reserve a little and then add the rest if the mixture appears a little stiff. You will find the mixture wetter than a cake made with traditional creaming or rubbing in methods – it is more like a batter. You could leave out the apples and fold in a few extra nuts which would provide an interesting alternative. It is good enough to double up as a pudding if you serve it with Greek yoghurt or fromage frais, or even an all-in-one custard sauce.

MAKES 1 × 20 cm (8 in) CAKE

100 g (4 oz) pecan nuts or
walnuts, roughly chopped
75 g (3 oz) demerara sugar
100 g (4 oz) soft margarine
150 g (5 oz) caster sugar
3 eggs
150 ml (5 fl oz) dry cider

225 g (8 oz) wholemeal self-
raising flour
1 teaspoon mixed spice
1 teaspoon baking powder
1 teaspoon bicarbonate of soda
2 cooking apples, peeled,
cored and sliced

Pre-heat the oven to gas mark 4, 180°C (350°F) and grease and line a 20 cm (8 in) deep cake tin.

Combine the nuts and demerara sugar. Place margarine, caster sugar, eggs, 100 ml (4 fl oz) of the cider, the sieved flour, mixed spice, baking powder and bicarbonate of soda in a large mixing bowl. Mix together well until you have a smooth batter – if the mixture is a little stiff, add the remaining cider. Place half the cake mixture in the lined cake tin. Cover with half the apples, plus half the nut and sugar mixture. Turn the remaining cake mixture into the tin. Spread the remaining apple slices over the top of the cake and sprinkle with remaining nuts and sugar. Bake in the oven for about 1 hour until risen, browned and set.

To freeze: cool, wrap and freeze for up to 3 months.
To defrost: overnight at cool room temperature.

Stocks and Sauces

Although stock cubes are a convenient short-cut to the lengthy process of stock-making they tend to be salty, and some brands can be quite synthetic in taste. I prefer the more robust flavour of a real home-made stock. I have therefore included recipes for a selection of home-made stocks; they do freeze well, so if you do find yourself with some time, a stock is well worth the extra effort. If you don't have the time, try out different stock cubes or concentrated stock until you find one you like.

I have also included some quick toppings for my ice-creams and some quick salad dressings.

Brown Bone Stock

MAKES ABOUT 2 litres (3½ pints)

1.5 kg (3 lb) beef bones	1 large bouquet garni
2 onions, quartered	6 peppercorns
2 carrots	2.25 litres (4 pints) water
1 stick celery, sliced	

Place the bones in a large pan over a gentle heat. Fry gently for 10 minutes. Add the vegetables and fry for a further 10 minutes until just coloured. Add the herbs, peppercorns and water. The water should come up two-thirds above the level of the ingredients. Bring to boil slowly, skimming occasionally. Half cover the pan to allow reduction to take place and simmer for 4 to 5 hours until the stock is reduced by half or tastes strong. Strain and cool to use for casseroles, sauces, gravies and soups.

To freeze: cool quickly then freeze in rigid containers for up to 4 months.
To defrost: overnight at cool room temperature. Re-heat thoroughly.

Rich Vegetable Stock

MAKES ABOUT 2 litres (3½ pints)

2 carrots, chopped	1 bouquet garni
3 potatoes, chopped	2 bay leaves
2 onions, chopped	8 black peppercorns
25 g (1 oz) mushroom stalks	1 ripe tomato, chopped
2 sticks celery, chopped	1.75 litres (3 pints) water
Salt	

Place all the ingredients in a large saucepan and bring to boil. Simmer very gently, uncovered, for 1½ to 2 hours until the vegetables are very tender. Strain through a sieve into a large bowl in batches, pressing through as many vegetables as possible. Leave until cold.

To freeze: cool then freeze in rigid containers for up to 4 months. To defrost: overnight at cool room temperature.

Chicken Stock

MAKES ABOUT 2 litres (3½ pints)

1 chicken carcass or chicken scraps
1 onion, peeled and sliced
1 carrot, sliced
1 stick celery, sliced
6 black peppercorns
1 bouquet garni
1.75 litres (3 pints) water

Place all the ingredients in a large saucepan. Bring to the boil. Using a slotted draining spoon, skim off any scum that forms on the surface of the liquid. Half cover and simmer gently for about 2 hours. Strain the stock into a bowl and leave to cool. Skim off any fat which forms on the surface of the stock. Use the stock as a base for sauces and soups.

To freeze: cool then freeze in rigid containers for up to 4 months. To defrost: overnight at cool room temperature. Re-heat thoroughly.

French Dressing

MAKES 250 ml (8 fl oz)

175 ml (6 fl oz) olive oil
4 tablespoons white wine vinegar
1 teaspoon French mustard
1 clove garlic, peeled and crushed
1 teaspoon runny honey
Salt and freshly ground black pepper

Place all the ingredients in a screw-topped jar and give a really good shake. Taste the dressing and season with salt and pepper if necessary. Keep the jar in the fridge whilst not in use.

This recipe is not suitable for freezing.

Mayonnaise

❖

Using the food processor makes mayonnaise-making simple and – dare I say it – foolproof.

MAKES 600 ml (1 pint)

2 eggs	1 tablespoon wine or cider
1 teaspoon salt	vinegar
Freshly ground black pepper	600 ml (1 pint) vegetable oil
1 teaspoon made mustard	Juice of 1 lemon
1 teaspoon caster sugar	

Place all the ingredients except the oil and lemon juice in a food processor or blender. Process for 2 to 3 minutes then, with the motor still running, add the oil in a slow thin stream until you have a thick sauce. You may not need all the oil. Add the lemon juice. Process again briefly. Check and adjust the seasoning to taste.

This recipe is not suitable for freezing.

Quick Fudge Sauce

❖

MAKES 350 ml (12 fl oz)

150 g (5 oz) soft light brown sugar	50 g (2 oz) butter or margarine
1 × 175 g (6 oz) tin evaporated milk	

Place all the ingredients in a saucepan and heat gently until the sugar has dissolved. Remember to keep the heat low. Bring to the boil for about 5 minutes. Pour into a jug. Cool and use to top ice-creams and sorbets.

This recipe is not suitable for freezing.

Bitter chocolate sauce

To serve with ice-cream.

MAKES ABOUT 300 ml (½ pint)

100 g (4 oz) good quality plain chocolate	**1 teaspoon instant coffee powder**
120 ml (4 fl oz) cold water	**1 teaspoon caster sugar**
50 g (2 oz) granulated sugar	

Gently melt the chocolate with the water, granulated sugar and coffee powder. Stir over a low heat until completely smooth.

Pour the sauce into a bowl and sprinkle with the caster sugar. Leave to cool. Stir well before serving hot or cold.

This recipe is not suitable for freezing.

Quick Tomato Sauce

MAKES ABOUT 450 ml (15 fl oz)

1 × 400 g (14 oz) tin tomatoes, drained	**A pinch of dried basil**
1 teaspoon tomato purée	**A pinch of sugar**
1 small onion, peeled and chopped	**Freshly ground black pepper**
1 clove garlic, peeled and crushed	**1 tablespoon vegetable oil**

Place all the ingredients in a food processor or blender and process until smooth. Heat in a medium saucepan until slightly thickened. Serve with pasta, or add to casseroles for an extra special kick.

This recipe is not suitable for freezing.

Sun-Dried Tomato Pasta Sauce

MAKES ABOUT 750 ml (1¼ pints)

75 g (3 oz) onion, peeled and coarsely chopped

75 g (3 oz) celery, coarsely chopped

75 g (3 oz) carrots, coarsely chopped

100 g (4 oz) sun-dried tomatoes in olive oil, drained

1½ tablespoons oil from the jar of tomatoes

1 clove garlic, peeled and crushed

25 g (1 oz) butter or margarine

1 × 400 g (14 oz) tin chopped tomatoes, drained

120 ml (4 fl oz) dry white wine

Salt and freshly ground black pepper

Place the onions, celery, carrots, sun-dried tomatoes, garlic, butter or margarine and oil in a saucepan. Cook the vegetables together for about 10 minutes until they are beginning to soften. Stir in the canned tomatoes and wine and season with salt and pepper. Simmer for about 25 minutes, uncovered. Place half the sauce in a food processor or blender and process until smooth. Then stir into the remaining sauce. Serve this lovely sauce over pasta, sprinkled with Parmesan cheese.

This recipe is not suitable for freezing.

Index